Glad I Didn't Know

Praise for *GLAD I DIDN'T KNOW*

According to social scientists, there is an anxiety epidemic in our country today. Yet in Scripture, Jesus constantly told his disciples, "Do not be afraid." You see, God never promised our lives would be free of hardship, but He did promise to walk through those valleys with us and use them for good. In *Glad I Didn't Know*, Vonna Laue takes us on a journey from anxiety in our lives to trust in our God, who sees and knows what we do not. *Glad I Didn't Know* will lift your spirits, make you laugh, and encourage you to let go of your fears and entrust them to Jesus. You'll want to read it at least twice—and maybe twice a year!

-**Richard Stearns,** President Emeritus of World Vision US, author of *Lead Like It Matters to God* and *The Hole in Our Gospel.*

In Vonna Laue's book, *Glad I Didn't Know,* she connects us to the real-life situations that we all face at some time or another. It's those times when love, care, and commitment meet us with a timeline that never aligns with ours, and the sacrifice of the situation can't be anticipated or measured until you are on the other side. Through her stories and those of others, she pulls from a deep well of experiences. Full of candor and truth, we find that even the most challenging roads are marked with hope. If you are heading into it, in the middle of it, or viewing life from the other side, *Glad I Didn't Know* will touch your heart and encourage you to give thanks and keep going!

-**Tami Heim,** President and CEO of Christian Leadership Alliance

God makes wonderful promises about our future but leaves out a lot of details we would like to know. Thank God for both—be glad about the promises and glad not to know the details.

-**Leith Anderson,** President Emeritus, National Association of Evangelicals, Washington, DC

Glad I Didn't Know is a deeply human reminder of how finite and small we are. Vonna Laue does an excellent job of weaving together stories from people in all stages of life, reminding us that none of us know what tomorrow will bring. Through each story and the principles learned, your faith will be strengthened and your discipleship deepened. Vonna's book puts our lives into God's perspective and helps us find joy as we receive the plan that God has for our lives, even when we don't know what that plan is.

-**Justin Burkholder,** International Director of TEAM

GLAD I DIDN'T KNOW

Lessons Learned Through

Life's Challenges

and Unexpected Blessings

VONNA LAUE

NASHVILLE

NEW YORK • LONDON • MELBOURNE • VANCOUVER

Glad I Didn't Know

Lessons Learned Through Life's Challenges and Unexpected Blessings

Published in New York, New York, by Morgan James Publishing. Morgan James is a trademark of Morgan James, LLC. www.MorganJamesPublishing.com

Proudly distributed by Publishers Group West®

Morgan James BOGO™

A **FREE** ebook edition is available for you or a friend with the purchase of this print book.

CLEARLY SIGN YOUR NAME ABOVE

Instructions to claim your free ebook edition:
1. Visit MorganJamesBOGO.com
2. Sign your name CLEARLY in the space above
3. Complete the form and submit a photo of this entire page
4. You or your friend can download the ebook to your preferred device

ISBN 9781636984629 paperback
ISBN 9781636984636 ebook
Library of Congress Control Number: 2024934062

Cover Design by:
Rachel Lopez
www.r2cdesign.com

Interior Design by:
Christopher Kirk
www.GFSstudio.com

Morgan James is a proud partner of Habitat for Humanity Peninsula and Greater Williamsburg. Partners in building since 2006.

Get involved today! Visit: www.morgan-james-publishing.com/giving-back

To my amazing family—so many of these stories are "our stories."
We have walked them together,
and I am blessed that God has given us each other.
I love you!

Contents

Introduction

'm a self-proclaimed control freak. Maybe you are too. I plan and then expect things to go according to that plan. If they don't, I'm disappointed and sometimes even grumpy.

I love being a mother and count it an immense privilege to have raised our two amazing daughters with my husband. However, I also enjoy my work and am grateful that our family situation allowed my husband to stay home with the girls. He has always been a great balance of nurture and discipline. I half-heartedly joke that I would have ruined them because I don't understand why a two-year-old can't sort their closet by short-sleeved shirts, long-sleeved shirts, pants, skirts, and dresses.

I give the above example to show that I am not kidding when I say I like order and control, but that's not how the Lord works. I can't recall a Scripture that refers to us taking control of our lives. There are many passages that indicate we are to relinquish control and have faith. Because of this struggle, an important passage for me has long been found in James 4:13–15.

> "Now listen, you who say, 'Today or tomorrow we will go to this or that city, spend a year there, carry on business and make money.' Why you do not even know what will happen tomorrow. What is your life? You are a mist that appears for a little while and then vanishes. Instead, you ought to say, 'If it is the Lord's will, we will live and do this or that.'"

The idea for this book began when a significant and unplanned transition happened in our lives that you will read more about later. I was surprised and extremely disappointed. God had blessed us in amazing ways, and then it seemed as if He changed the rules in the middle of the game, just when we were winning. I questioned why He would have put us in this circumstance when it could have been easily avoided if He hadn't led us in that direction just eighteen months before. Then I thought about a couple of byproducts from the original decision that was clearly God-led and realized I was glad I didn't know the outcome ahead of time—because I wouldn't have been obedient.

I considered other circumstances in my life when I was glad I didn't know the outcome because those times were painful, and I wouldn't have willingly subjected myself to them. I realized the Lord worked "for the good" in each of those situations. After a period of contemplating several challenges in life, I considered the really good things that happened and again realized I was glad I didn't know those outcomes beforehand. I would have tried to take control and orchestrate the result and quite simply would have messed it all up.

You see, the Lord doesn't need you or me to take care of the details. He needs us to trust Him. He needs us to clearly understand that faith shows up in the things we don't see and not in the things we do, as is made clear in Hebrews 11:1: "Now faith is the substance of things hoped for, the evidence of things not seen" (KJV).

Each set of life's circumstances causes me to have greater faith. I can look back and see how the Lord was in the middle of every situation. The phrase "Hindsight is 20/20" certainly applies to your faith journey and mine. I usually can't see it when I'm in the middle of a decision or challenge, but faith is like a muscle that gets stronger each time it is exercised. If I can calm down and step back, I realize He has brought me through so many things in the past that the current set of circumstances are not insurmountable.

I used to be a "Here's my plan, Lord. Just sign here, and I'll be on my way. You don't even need to worry about reading through it. I've got this. There is no need for me to bother you" kind of person. I realized a few years ago that if the Lord had only given me what I asked for or what I considered, I would have missed out on many amazing opportunities and blessings in life. So I have moved on to say, "Lord, I have faith in your plans. Please reveal them to me." I tend to add, "But please tell me right now what that is." I figure if I live another three or four decades, I may be able to honestly say, "Lord, your will be done in your time."

I'm just not there yet. Baby steps.

In the pages ahead, you will walk through some of the **"Glad I Didn't Know"** moments in the lives of several people. My prayer is that as you read these, you'll consider your circumstances or life stories and create your own **"Glad I Didn't Know"** list. As you assemble that list of difficulties and tragedies—as well as triumphs and blessings—may you grow closer to the Lord and understand His deep, deep love for you and know without a doubt that He truly *is* working all things together for good, as it says in Romans 8:28.

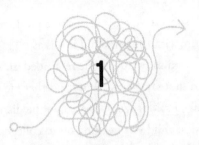

Quit a Job, Flood a House, Lose a Parent

The year 2016 didn't start in any remarkable way. I began serving on the board of directors for World Vision US and was excited about that. Work had your basic struggles that exist in any leadership role, but I loved the people I worked most closely with and loved the clients we served. Our girls were doing well, and we were your typical American family, with two kids and a dog (the most adorable English bulldog ever).

As summer approached, I began to have a level of unrest or lack of contentment related to my work. I sensed the Lord saying my time at the accounting firm for which I worked was coming to an end. I ignored it because this work had been so important to me. The prodding continued. Bryan and I discussed it and decided we would come back to the discussion after we returned from a trip to Kenya, which our family was taking to see the work World Vision was doing there in July.

When we returned, the sense of leaving was even stronger. We prayed about it, and ultimately, it seemed to us a matter of obedience. If I didn't step out in faith and leave my job, it would be detrimental to the firm and to our family. I argued with the Lord about this. If you haven't done that before, I don't suggest you try it. It's not productive. I told Him I was planning to retire with the firm, and it was as if He said, "So." Then I told Him it was economically stupid. He reminded me of the whole, "He owns the cattle on a thousand hills" thing and that He could take care of us financially. Finally, I said it would be okay if he disrupted Bryan's and my life, and our oldest child was heading off to college, but our youngest was just going into high school, so this was not a good time. He let me know that He didn't intend something for our good that would be for her bad. I lost the argument.

In the firm, I was required to give a one-year notice before leaving. I let the partners know I would be leaving at the end of the year and shared with them how it seemed to be a matter of obedience. For some people, giving a four-month notice is unimaginable, but for partners in a CPA firm, that is very little notice. I spent those four months transitioning clients and meeting with network connections to let them know I was leaving. I wanted to make sure I ended well and that it didn't have a negative impact on the firm. The first thing people wanted to know was what I was going to do, and this left-brained, analytical, type-A personality had to say, "I don't know." It was a really difficult thing to tell myself and others that I was stepping out in faith because I believed that was what the Lord was calling me to do.

Quitting my job was just the first step in a really difficult fall season full of change and lessons and growth. The week I let the firm know I would be leaving was the first week of our oldest daughter, Bethany's, senior season of high school volleyball. We have been a volleyball family through and through, and it is something that has brought us all together for many years. She was being recruited by a few colleges around the country, and we were excited about her possibilities as well as that of her team in this season. I won't give away what happened next, as our daughter tells the story in her own words in the next chapter. I will simply say it was a significant event for the year.

Two weeks later, while Bethany and Bryan were on a pre-planned recruiting trip, I decided Kimberly, our younger daughter, and I should go to the beach for the weekend. The beach is my happy place, and while Kimberly didn't love the beach itself, she could take a book and be happy anywhere.

We left on a Friday after school. As we took our bags to the vehicle, I walked past the water shutoff and thought about how Bryan always shut the water off when we left town for a trip. We were just going to be gone for the weekend, and I chose not to stop and do it. Big mistake!

We had a great weekend and returned early enough on Sunday morning to get ready and go to church. Kimberly got to the house first and opened the door. As I came down the sidewalk with my arms full, I heard a strange sound growing louder. When I got into the entryway and looked down the stairs to the main living level, I saw it was flooded. The sound was the awful hissing of water coming from a valve in the bathroom, where a gasket had given out and had been spraying water since shortly after we left two days before. I'm a pretty logical and methodical person, but I called Bryan, hysterical. He thought someone had died because I was so distraught. I didn't even know where to start. It ultimately resulted in about $60,000 worth of remodeling and four months of having to stay out of the main living area of our home.

Before fall was over, we had one more blow to our family. My stepdad passed away at the end of October. While his health had been poor for years, there was no indication that something would happen this suddenly, and we fully expected to all be together for Christmas as we had been every year before. He had been part of my life for nearly thirty-five years. My mom has always wished that we lived closer to her, but I had promised that if I was ever needed, I would be home ASAP. She called me on Saturday morning to tell me what had happened, and I was in her living room that evening. My family joined a couple of days later. We spent the next week laughing, crying, and making many decisions. Then my family returned to California, and my mom started a new journey as a widow.

In a matter of less than three months, I had quit my job, we had dealt with a major disappointment, our house had flooded, and we had lost a beloved family member. If you were to script your life, this is probably not how you would do it. The pain, strain, and uncertainty were constant and sometimes extreme.

Glad I Didn't Know

When I say, "I'm glad I didn't know," please understand that isn't always the literal case. I wish I had known the house would flood. I promise that I would have taken the extra thirty seconds to walk over and shut off the water before we left for the weekend. I am certainly glad I didn't know all of those things would happen in that time frame, though. The stress alone of knowing an avalanche like that was coming would have been too great. First Corinthians 10:13 says, "No temptation has overtaken you that is not common to man. God is faithful, and He will not let you be tempted beyond your ability, but with the temptation, He will also provide the way of escape, that you may be able to endure it" (NLT). While I read that as a promise that we won't be given more than we can handle, I have come to believe that sometimes, it may mean *not knowing what is ahead.*

Lesson Learned

As I write this and ponder the lessons, my first thought is, *Where do I start?* Most importantly, it is that God's plans continue to be so much better than my plans. We read that or hear that, but do we really *know* that? Let me explain how that was true in these situations.

Quitting my job: We ultimately moved to Virginia (which I also argued with the Lord about). That ended up being the perfect place for our youngest daughter to be for her high school years and set her up for the next phase of life in ways I could never have imagined. It also led to me start a consulting practice, which has become an absolute joy of mine.

House flooding: Remember the remodel costs I mentioned? They were covered by our homeowner's insurance. I enjoyed the beautiful changes for several months, but the best part was that when the Lord moved us out of state, we had a fully updated home when it went on the market to be sold.

Stepdad's death: We miss him, and we still laugh and tell stories about him, but he had been in poor health for a long time. He had been confined to home, and his passing took away that pain and suffering. It also provided my mom with the ability to do things in her life that she hadn't been able to do for quite a while.

> "For my thoughts are not your thoughts neither are your ways my ways, declares the Lord. As the heavens are higher than the earth, so are my ways higher than your ways and my thoughts than your thoughts" (Isaiah 55:8–9).

Questions to Consider

- Have you gone through a period in life when it seemed you were encountering one difficult event after another?

- What have you argued with the Lord about? How did it turn out?

- Are you holding on to something because you think you know how it will turn out and you're trying to control the outcome?

2

Money Shot

Bethany Donahue

I come from a sports family. There wasn't a time growing up that I remember not having some sport on television; fall was for football, late winter meant the start of NASCAR, and summer was a great opportunity to get out to the ballpark for a baseball game. Naturally, our love for sports meant that my desire to play on teams was fostered from a young age.

I remember five-year-old soccer games, complete with orange slices at halftime. Then I moved on to fourth-grade volleyball and half-pound bean burritos before games (who thought that was a good idea!?). Until eighth grade, I played basketball and volleyball, both sports advantageously geared toward my six-foot-tall frame.

However, when I got to eighth grade, I realized my basketball career may be impacted by the little fact that I couldn't make a basket—a fundamental part of the game! So I put my basketball shoes away, and on top of playing on my small Christian school's volleyball team that year, I asked my parents if I could join a travel volleyball club.

The club volleyball scene is competitive, especially in Southern California, but effectively geared toward helping players hone their skills to play at the collegiate level. Even after having to miss both high school and club seasons for a scoliosis-related back surgery during my freshman year, I came into my senior season having played nearly year-round for three years and was decidedly the best player on our team from our high school of eighty people.

We had the strong notion that this was going to be "our season." I was a team captain and had gone so far as posting the statistics of the league MVP from the previous season on the mirror in my bedroom, convinced the MVP would be me that year.

Our team practiced hard all summer and came into our first game of the season at the end of August with great anticipation and a good deal of optimism for the year ahead. The game began and, all was going well, our team demonstrating the hard work we had put in. Then, suddenly, on a routine hitting attack, I made my approach and jumped like I had thousands of times before. This time, however, upon landing, a piercing pain shot through my left knee, and I instantly crumpled to the hardwood floor.

My hands grasped my leg as my dad, one of our assistant coaches, came out to assess my injury. I could not bend my knee or put any weight on it. So we set up an appointment with an orthopedist for the next day. He sent me for an MRI and then gave us the results. The first film showed a strained MCL, which could be rehabbed. So far, not as bad as we thought. The next film showed a torn meniscus, and the surgeon told us this could easily be repaired. That sounded encouraging. Then he put up the third film and said, "Here's the money shot." It was a complete tear of the ACL, which confirmed what we'd all been suspecting but dreading: a season and high school career-ending injury.

It felt like a blow to not only my volleyball season but to a part of my identity. Volleyball was one of the things I held most dear, something I had worked on for years and planned for success for years to come. What would I do without it?

On top of that, I was in the final stages of the recruiting process with a couple of universities to play collegiately. How would this injury affect my prospects of receiving scholarships and playing the sport I loved at the next level?

My dad and I had a recruiting trip lined up for mid-September, just a couple of weeks after my injury. So we loaded my crutches and flew east—first to a school in South Carolina, then to Asbury University, in central Kentucky.

The first school was the one I had been most excited about. It was bigger, in a higher athletic division, and had given me the best impression on my first visit. However, when I returned for this second trip, everything about it felt wrong.

The meeting with the coach was discouraging; he insisted that, with the injury I had, I would need to switch positions, no longer playing middle blocker—the only position for which I had ever trained.

Dad and I left South Carolina the next day, both silently hoping things would go better in Kentucky . . . and they did. The meeting with Asbury's head coach was the opposite of the previous day's experience as he looked me in the eye and told me he knew I would put in the work to get back to full strength—and that there was still a place for me on Asbury's roster.

In addition, a family friend had lined up an opportunity for me to meet with the chair of Asbury's Christian Studies Department because I was interested in studying theology. That Saturday meeting, along with the athletic and academic scholarships Asbury laid out for me, cemented my decision to be an Eagle.

While the prospect of moving to Kentucky for college was exciting, it didn't change the fact that there were some very hard conditions about accepting a senior year that looked significantly different from what I expected. Rather than spending my senior season dominating our volleyball conference, I spent a good portion of it in the physical therapist's office, doing some of the most painful rehabilitation exercises out there.

During this time, I often asked the Lord, "Why me?" At the same time, the song *Thy Will* by Hillary Scott was released and seemed to play on the radio constantly. That song talks about being in a painful place after following the Lord's leading and not understanding the *why*. It is a poignant reminder that God sees the entire picture of our lives, and we must trust that He's using hardships for a purpose. It hit a bit too close to home as I processed how an injury that took away a volleyball season I had worked toward for a long time could possibly be used for good.

I am grateful the Lord doesn't let us off the hook easily. I continued to hear that song frequently throughout the year and had to learn to trust God and His promises over my feelings. Not playing volleyball that year also allowed me more time to invest in my school as I served as our student body chaplain and helped me say yes to some really great experiences with friends before we all left for college.

Graduation finally came and, in the fall of 2017, I packed my bags for Wilmore, Kentucky, moved into historic Glide Crawford Hall on the edge of Asbury's campus, and began four of the most transformational years of my life. I chose to study Bible Theology and Spanish with an interest in serving in ministry and possibly missions in the future.

I had chosen a Christian college for the many ways I knew I could grow spiritually: classes taught from a biblical perspective, chapel three times a week, and lots of Bible study opportunities. What I didn't expect or anticipate were all the new relationships God would bring into my life in that season and use to grow me and lead me toward the good future He had planned for me.

During my freshman year, I formed friendships with four students who had lived in East Africa during their childhoods. As someone interested in missions in the future, but with no personal experience or background in what that life involved, hearing the stories of these missionary kids was so impactful as I processed with the Lord what He was calling me to do. By the end of my freshman year, I could confidently say I was open to missions if the Lord led me there.

These same friends introduced me to a student center on campus that hosted a worship service and dinner every Sunday night centered around missions and what God was doing around the world. I attended every week and gradually began spending time there midweek as well. God used these services and a mission trip through the center to definitively call me to serve in the mission field.

He also used the student center as the place where he introduced me to my husband. During my junior year, I joined the student leadership team that helped plan and execute the missions services. Andrés was a shy and kind missionary kid from Paraguay who also served on the team as our tech person. Through time and proximity, God brought our hearts together. We started dating that same year and got married the November after I graduated.

Now, as Andrés and I have just welcomed our first child together, live and do ministry in a multicultural neighborhood thirty minutes away from the school that brought us together, and prepare to follow God's calling to serve in Paraguay on the mission field where he grew up, I am amazed at the God who takes difficult circumstances and uses them for His glory.

Glad I Didn't Know

Of course, I would have never chosen a torn ACL. Now, I cannot imagine how my life would have turned out without that fateful jump.

I am almost certain I would not have attended Asbury if not for my injury. Had I not attended Asbury, so much about my life would be different now. I would not live in Kentucky, where I have a wonderful church community and relationships that have formed me in many ways.

I would not have met my husband or had my son. I might not have ever heard of Paraguay, much less be preparing to take the gospel to the unreached people of that nation as a missionary.

I am convinced that life with God is a great adventure, and the best thing we can do is keep saying yes to Him. However, if I could have seen all of the circumstances that played into my journey ahead of time, I promise you that I would've tried to manipulate them to avoid pain—every time. In doing so, I would've missed out on some of the greatest adventures God has led me on.

Lessons Learned

We serve a loving God. In this season, I learned the meaning of Romans 8:28, that God makes all things work together for good. That verse doesn't mean God *makes* all things happen. I don't believe He directly caused my ACL to rupture. He allowed it, though. Working things for the good of His people isn't defined by our standards. Good is defined by an all-knowing, all-powerful God who can see far beyond our current circumstances.

We live in a broken world, where painful and sometimes tragic events befall us. I was fortunate that, for me, it was just a knee. So many have it much worse. However, the hope and promise of the gospel is that our God can always turn tragedy to work for His purposes and glory, and He doesn't let any experience get wasted if we let Him move in our lives.[1]

> "And we know that in all things God works for the good of those who love him, who have been called according to his purpose" (Romans 8:28).

---

1   Bethany Donahue has served in college campus ministry and church ministry since graduating from Asbury University with a degree in Bible Theology and Spanish. She and her husband, Andrés, enjoy raising their family together and serving in multicultural ministries wherever the Lord leads them.

Questions to Consider

- Out of what painful or negative circumstances in your life have you seen God work out something good?

- Was there something in which you invested years of your life or many resources that was then suddenly taken away?

- How does the promise that God works *all* things for good impact the way you live in seasons of hardship?

Lost, Lonely, Broke

Edgar Sandoval Sr.

The 500-degree grill and sizzling, popping grease were not the problem. In my polyester uniform and paper hat, I could flip burgers all day long over the bright orange flames. No, the problem was the burger orders, coming rapid-fire from the cashier over the tinny kitchen speakers.

I was eighteen and had recently moved to New Jersey after spending most of my life—twelve years—in Venezuela. Although I had been born in the US and was a full-fledged citizen, Spanish was my mother tongue. As I painfully experienced at Burger King, the only thing more frustrating than being unable to speak the language in a new place is being unable to understand it.

You would think I would have been assigned to do something that didn't require much English. But no, my boss put me to work on the grill, taking verbal orders from the cashiers. Here's how it would go: the cashier would joyfully ask for the patron's order, and then he would turn around toward the kitchen and give me a menacing look that said, *See if you can understand this.* And my agony would start as I tried to discern what he was saying.

Most of the time, this is what I heard: "Whopper with hamana, hamana, hamana, hamana, and hamana mayo." Desperately, I wondered, *Was that hold the cheese or double cheese, extra pickles or no pickles, and was that heavy mayo or hold the mayo?* Followed by the frantic thought, *I can't be fired! I need this job!*

Across from me, working the other side of the grill, was Lorraine, a fifty-year-old woman whom the Lord had blessed with all senses except one: the sense of urgency. Lorraine made one burger per eight-hour shift. But she spoke English, so when those orders came, I would look at Lorraine and ask her, "Lorraine, what say?" She'd only shrug.

It was a nightmare. I forced myself to remember my mom's words: "*Al mal tiempo, buena cara.*" In bad times, let your best face show. And now, I can look back on this season and laugh. Burger King's advertising slogan at the time was "Have it your way," but while I was on the grill, I fulfilled most orders *my* way!

In the end, I turned my trial into triumph at Burger King. After months of improving my English, working hard, and "letting my best face show" with cruel cashiers and coworkers like Lorraine, I achieved a role I had only dreamed of . . . taking orders at the drive-through window!

The minimum-wage jobs I did in that period of my life—flipping burgers, as well as bagging groceries and mopping floors at a grocery store—are a common rite of passage for American kids. Likewise, they were necessary for me to reach my goal of attending a good college. I didn't mind working hard, but at the time, my life was unrecognizable compared to what I thought it would be.

In Venezuela, where my Guatemalan parents had moved our family when I was six, I'd had a great childhood. We lived in La Victoria, a town about an hour west of Caracas. My dad worked as a production manager in a factory. Our neighborhood was like Disney's Epcot Center, with many nationalities, languages, and cultures represented. All the residents banded together and became inseparable. Our parents created a social club called *Amistad* 70 (Friendship 70), and we spent holidays and significant events together, including Christmas, birthdays, and weddings. I had a wide, diverse circle of friends.

In school, I was a high achiever, earning good grades while participating in all the activities. My dream in high school was to become an engineer, *Ingeniero Sandoval!* I set my sights on attending the top engineering school in the country, Simon Bolivar University. By my senior year, my plan was taking shape; I was accepted by the university and plotted a move to Caracas, where my life as an adult would really begin.

Then, in just a few months, everything changed. My father lost his job, and the bottom fell out of our finances. We sold off our assets to pay rent and keep food on the table. My parents fought, then separated. With the breakdown of my family and the increasing presence of hunger as an unwelcome guest in our household, I needed to rapidly and radically revise my plans.

The only sensible thing to do was leave Venezuela, move back to the US, and try to restart my life. So I took (and aced) my final exams, skipped my high school graduation, and boarded a plane with my mom to her native country, Guatemala. There, my aunts bought me a plane ticket to the US.

That's how I found myself arriving in New York alone at age eighteen. I carried everything I owned in my dad's green Army duffle bag, with my American passport in one pocket and $50 in the other.

In New Jersey, I lived with my sister in a basement apartment where the hot-water pipes made such a racket in the wintertime that I feared someone was trying to break in. Our food budget was $13 a week, not a penny more.

While I didn't think it would be easy to start over in an unfamiliar country, I had always pictured America as most of the world does, as "the land of opportunity." I was a bright kid and ready to work hard, and I had the all-important US passport to pave my way.

The reality was a shock. I felt like an immigrant in my own country. Communicating was a constant struggle. I was clueless about American customs and traditions. The first time I was invited to Thanksgiving dinner, I looked at the turkey and thought, *Wow, that is a really big chicken!*

The worst part was battling perception versus reality. Many people didn't see me as the college-bound young man who had scored at the top of his high school class. They saw me working minimum wage jobs, heard my broken English, and made certain assumptions about me.

This continued even when I reached my goal: admission to Rutgers University. I was excited to enroll specifically in the engineering school, but the admissions counselor told me my SAT scores weren't good enough. I tried to explain the test in English had been too challenging for me to understand and complete in time. I said I could show her my high school scores and prove I'd been accepted into the best engineering school in Venezuela, but she interrupted me. "Study sociology," she said, explaining that if I did well in the School of the Arts, perhaps I could apply to the School of Engineering later. Then she told me not to get my hopes up. In her experience, chances were low that I would make it. In retrospect, I realized she wasn't really seeing me and my potential—only my circumstances.

I walked out of the office dejected, as if the rug had been pulled out from under my feet—again! That disappointing exchange with the admissions counselor was a rocky beginning to my time at Rutgers, but it would not define the journey or the ending. I worked hard and made lifelong friends. I found mentors and coaches among my professors and counselors, those who never let me give up on my dreams.

Yes, I studied sociology. But when I graduated from Rutgers in 1989, it was with a Bachelor of Arts in Sociology *and* a Bachelor of Science in Engineering, plus a minor in math, with honors! I was recruited by General Electric and worked for three years there as an engineer. Then I decided to try something new, so I went for my MBA at the Wharton School of Business at the University of Pennsylvania.

In 1994, I joined Procter & Gamble, the largest consumer goods company in the world, and started climbing the corporate ladder. Over the next twenty years, I earned promotions and higher leadership positions, including marketing director, North America Fabric Care; vice president, North America Marketing, and vice president and general manager of Global Feminine Care.

P&G shaped me into the leader I always wanted to be. It wasn't until 2002, though, when I surrendered my heart to Jesus, that I realized all along, God was shaping me into the leader *He* wanted me to be. After all, He had a special assignment prepared for me: president and chief executive officer of World Vision, the largest Christian organization in the United States—the role I assumed in 2018.

Glad I Didn't Know

I'm glad I didn't know what my life would be like in America when I left Venezuela at eighteen. How much harder everything is when you don't know the language. How unfashionable the polyester fast-food uniform is, especially the paper hat! Seriously . . . had I known how lost, lonely, and broke I would feel, I never would have wanted to get on that plane.

The experience gave me an insight I never would have learned another way: nobody wants to leave the people they love and the place they know. More than 100 million people are currently displaced from their homes, forced to make an impossible choice to leave. My situation was a far cry from the reasons many people flee, such as the horrors of war or, as is happening now in Venezuela, total economic collapse.

Around the globe, World Vision serves refugees, migrants, and displaced people, equipping them with practical help and hope. I've visited several of the world's largest refugee settlements, and when I share with supporters or the media the heartbreaking stories of the people I've met, it is with special empathy—because I have made that difficult choice myself.

Also, even as I struggled, I never knew that I was poor, as incredible as that sounds! Twenty years after graduating from Rutgers, I was invited back to give a commencement speech. My former advisor asked me to meet with Education Opportunity Fund (EOF) students, a group I had been a part of when I attended Rutgers. I asked her what the criteria were for EOF. She hemmed and hawed before admitting that it was for students below the poverty line. So I *was* poor, but I'm glad I didn't know it. Poverty can be a self-limiting mindset. No matter how broke I sometimes felt, I always considered myself wealthy in potential and drive.

Lessons Learned

In my first years in America, I learned the importance of having a dream and being willing to sacrifice to achieve it. I tell my kids that if their dream is the "what," sacrifice is the "how." No matter what life throws at you, do what you must to keep focused on your dream. As my mom instilled, let your best face show!

I also learned how critical it is to look at *who* a person truly is, beyond their circumstances. We are each created in God's image, full of potential, and with a purpose He intends for us. I've met many children around the world who are intelligent, creative, and resourceful. Their circumstances may limit them, but they don't define them. Everyone deserves the chance I was given to prove who I really was and live into my God-given purpose.

My greatest lesson is that God works in the twists and turns of our lives. He is *always* working in us, especially during unexpected changes and painful experiences. When I look back, I realize He was protecting me and preparing me for where I am today—leading a ministry focused on empowering the world's most vulnerable people.

For example . . .

- As a teenager, experiencing the hardship of not knowing where my next meal was coming from gave me empathy for the many vulnerable children and families around the world for whom hunger is a daily reality. I know from my own experience they need more than physical help; they also need the hope of Christ.
- Feeling like an immigrant in my own country—starting over in an unfamiliar and unwelcoming place, where you're not treated the same as others and you have to work twice as hard for everything—gave me special empathy for the plight of refugees and displaced people.
- As a young man, being smart and ambitious but having all the odds stacked against me helps me identify strongly with the kids I've met in my travels who are gifted, full of potential, and who just need an opportunity and someone to believe in them. That's what World Vision child sponsorship aims to do for millions of children.

Seeing God's hand in the trials of my life has given me unshakeable trust in His faithfulness. He is always with me, leading me where He wants me to go.[2]

---

2   Edgar Sandoval Sr. is president and CEO of World Vision. He brings to the role a deep Christian faith commitment, innovative leadership experience, and an understanding of other cultures after living in South and Central America. Under his leadership, World Vision has raised record-breaking donations, impacting millions more children and families living in poverty.

"Trust in the Lord with all your heart and lean not on your own understanding; in all your ways submit to him, and he will make your paths straight" (Proverbs 3:5-6).

Questions to Consider

- What have you learned from achieving goals that were nearly impossible to reach versus those that came easily?

- Reflecting on any struggles you've had in your past, do you think you would be the same person without them? Would you be the person God intends for you to be?

- Looking back on your life, how have you seen God's guiding hand in the twists and turns that have led you to where you are today?

4

D-I-V-O-R-C-E

For those of you who believe in personality types based on birth order, I am an only child. I know what you are thinking. There are good characteristics like independence and leadership, but we are also known for being spoiled and wanting to be the center of attention. Now, let me add that my parents divorced when I was eight, and both remarried within two years, making me a middle child in two families. Those kids are often people pleasers and peacemakers who sometimes feel left out. Let's finish that off by telling you that my dad remarried again after I was an adult with my own family, and I became the baby of a family with two step-siblings, one of whom I'd never met in person. Wow! Have I thoroughly confused you about my personality?

Children don't know what is ahead for them and neither do they get to choose it. I grew up in a small town in South Dakota. I sometimes say I grew up in rural South Dakota, and a friend teases me by saying, "Isn't that redundant?" It was a good place to grow up, and there is often a strong work ethic when you come from a rural part of the country. I appreciate the opportunities I had as a child and know they are part of what makes me who I am today.

For part of my younger years, my dad was a police officer and my mom was a police dispatcher. This meant they both worked shift work, and they rarely worked the same shift. I remember some days—maybe a Tuesday, for example—I would say, "For my mom, it's Monday, and for my dad, it's Friday." That really confused people, but it was completely logical to my six-year-old brain.

I won't delve into many specifics of my parent's relationship out of respect for them and their privacy. However, some aspects impacted who I am today—as is the case with every person. Our home was a volatile place. I was not injured, but you never knew what was going to erupt and when. I couldn't have friends over. There were neighbor kids, and we played outside, or I would go to their house so I wasn't isolated, but it wasn't possible to invite anyone to my house. I wasn't a middle child yet, but I still tried to be a people pleaser and a peacemaker, a little kid just hoping there wouldn't be another fight.

I also realized as an adult that I have very few memories from when I was a kid. I remember the popcorn balls that my friend's grandma gave out at Halloween, and I remember playing several games or sports with friends in the street, which was perfectly acceptable in the '70s. I don't remember Christmases or any time spent together with my parents. I don't remember birthdays, and according to my grandma and my aunt, my birthday was forgotten one year. It didn't impact me greatly because I don't remember that, either.

My childhood was not miserable. My mom and dad loved me dearly and have my entire life. It was, however, difficult and not ideal. When my husband and I started dating, I was in high school and had no idea how to argue. He had such a different perspective. If we had a disagreement, I thought our relationship was over. His attitude after we talked it through was, "So we had a fight. Let's go get ice cream." I'm so thankful for the family structure he had, though I know he would say that his wasn't perfect either.

As a child, I thought, *My family is so dysfunctional!* I tried to hide it because I didn't want people to find out how different I was, or how *weird* my family was. What took me years to understand was that all families have dysfunction. It just looks different from one family to the next. Even my husband's family, whom I love and adore, has some dysfunction you could find if you looked. As we have our own family now, I just like to say, "It is part of our charm."

Glad I Didn't Know

As a child, I'm glad I didn't know what the next day would hold. I lived in the moment, which allowed me to cope with the present situation. I'm glad I didn't know that I would meet and marry Bryan. I would never have thought I was good enough to be part of his family. I didn't know in advance, and it happened before I had the opportunity to get scared and run away. Though, frankly, I tried a few times! Bryan kept loving me and showing me trust and security. I'm glad I didn't know we would have such amazing kids. I would have felt inadequate to raise these terrific girls. I also would have panicked about what we needed to do to get them to this point when all we needed to do was parent them, pray, and entrust them to the Lord.

Family means different things to different people and in different seasons. I'm glad I didn't know what it would mean because I can see God's hand of protection and direction through it all.

Lessons Learned

My life has been impacted by my childhood and my parents' divorce in several ways. I have always wanted our kids to invite people to our house. I want them to enjoy being with us. When they were younger, I wanted to have kids in our home who didn't have the security our girls had. They may have needed, even if only for a couple of hours, to have somewhat of an example of a stable home.

I fly frequently, and near the holidays and in the summer, I find there is a specific population of passengers who don't fly at other times. Those are the children of divorced parents who, through custody arrangements and distance, have to fly to spend time with either their mom or dad. My heart goes out to them, and I honestly pray for each of them when I see that situation. I understand how they hurt because they can't just be together like a "normal" family.

We have traditions, and we spend time together as a family. There are many traditions in our home around Christmas. If you ever want to hear about them, just ask me. I'm always thrilled to discuss them at length. We have chili and cornbread every Halloween. Bryan would carve pumpkins with the girls, and we did an annual photo with their costumes and the pumpkins. There was the first day of school photo every year and the eating of junk food all day long on New Year's Day while we watched the Rose Parade and football. These traditions are not just routines I won't change; they are a way of connecting us and creating memories, which I now find are outlasting the times when we aren't physically in the same house.

We were blessed to travel and vacation a lot with our girls (still do!). Sometimes they thought it was great, and sometimes they were bored—like the trip we did to several national parks, culminating at the Grand Canyon, where they are quoted saying, "More rocks?!" I loved having dinner together as often as possible around our busy schedules, which meant for quite a while, we would go out on Sunday night. When we got home from dinner, we had a family meeting to go through the hectic schedule of the week ahead. I'm famous in our house (and frequently mocked) for saying, "Together as a family."

I've also learned we are part of various families. You may also have a work family or a church family. I'm so thankful for the various families we are a part of, whether chosen for us or chosen by us. The role we play in each of these situations is an opportunity to be Christ to others.

> "'I will be a Father to you, and you will be my sons and daughters,' says the Lord Almighty" (2 Corinthians 6:18).

Questions to Consider

- How has your childhood family life impacted the way you respond to situations now?

- Are there ways your current family life can be a blessing to others?

- What are you glad you didn't know related to family?

5

The Sandwich Generation

A s an only child, there are times when I know it would be helpful to have a sibling, for example, to help care for aging parents. It would be nice to go on vacation and ask someone else to be "on call" for our parents' needs. I realize, in many families, that responsibility still falls primarily on one person, so I can appreciate the positive aspects of being an only child. When a decision needs to be made, I make it, and there is no one to argue or disagree with me (except, of course, the involved parent).

As an adult, I have discovered that divorce doesn't just impact children when they are kids. It follows them through the rest of their lives. A primary example happened a few years ago. My dad's required level of care increased to the point that he needed to move to a new assisted living facility. It made sense to make the transition from Iowa (where he lived) to Virginia, to be closer to me. However, my mom still lived in South Dakota.

My mom had experienced a serious accident with her horse, which required two surgeries, five days in the ICU, and nearly a month in the hospital. I was there for most of that time as well as the time it took to get her settled back at home and take care of the five chickens, four horses, three cats, and two dogs. Though, by the time I was done, there were only four chickens. Don't ask. I don't know where the other one went. I thought they were all allowed to be out of their coop during the day. Oops!

My dad had Parkinson's disease, cancer, and diabetes. He needed a significant amount of care, and I am very thankful for the two assisted living centers where he lived. When he found out about my mom's accident, he asked what he could do. Realistically, there was nothing he could do, so I asked him to just work hard to take care of himself and get along with everyone where he lived to not create additional problems. It was a blessing that Bryan took him to his three appointments that month. I simply couldn't deal with the tag-team needs they could encounter 1,500 miles apart.

Not only am I an only child, but so was my father. At one point, I found myself in a situation where my dad was in assisted living and my grandpa was still living in his own house. I had always told him that I would help him anytime he needed anything. He was a proud German and wouldn't accept help unless no other option existed. So when he called me one day in February and said he needed help—needed to go into an assisted living facility right away—I dropped everything and flew across the country to help. For the next four months, I traveled to him to get him settled. I also traveled to Iowa to pick up my dad and drive him to South Dakota to see his dad.

It has always been a balancing act to be a wife and mother and still be available for the needs of my parents and grandparents. They talk about the sandwich generation, and during those years of being concerned over the needs of grandparents as well, I told people I was more like a McDonald's Big Mac with a third bun!

I have found in parenting children, you can, and often should, tell them what to do. In caring for parents, you may know what is needed, but there is still the aspect of honoring your parents, which significantly complicates things. How do you honor them and yet influence them to make good decisions? Some days, I do it better than others. I tell our girls that I am doing my best to model how to care for my parents so, as they see me do it, they will be encouraged to care well for Bryan and me when we get older. Give us a few decades, and I will let you know if that worked or not.

Glad I Didn't Know

Raising parents and grandparents is like having children. Most people can slowly acclimate to it. You have one child and then later, another, and so on. We don't typically wake up one day and have two or three parents and a couple of grandparents who are pulling us in different directions.

I got on a 6 a.m. flight one day and reached for my phone to shut it off as the cabin door closed. It was ringing, and it was my dad. When I answered, he said he thought his wife had experienced a stroke. All I could say was, "If you're serious, then when I hang up, you need to dial 9-1-1. I'll call you back when I land." That was the start of a major life transition for everyone involved. His wife nearly died, went to a nursing home for rehab, and, ultimately, transferred to assisted living for the rest of her life. I found out Dad had been in the emergency room thirteen times in the five months leading up to the incident. I flew to be with them, and in one week, navigated the needs at the hospital as well as found an open assisted living facility where Dad could move. I also helped him move in before heading home to tend to my family and job.

I'm glad I didn't know what the needs would be and when. I would have wasted so much time trying to plan exactly how to handle all the details, causing me and those around me to miss out on opportunities because I had to hold things open for the crisis that was going to arise. The Lord is just what we need when we need it.

I'm glad I didn't know my mom would nearly die in a horse accident. I would have begged and hassled her to get rid of her horses. They are the biggest joys in her life, and she was back riding again within eight weeks of being in the ICU. It would have driven a wedge between us that might have been irreparable. The Lord gave me just what I needed, just when I needed it, to handle the situations.

Lessons Learned

On one of my many trips to Omaha, Nebraska, where I'd then drive to Sioux Center, Iowa, to pick up my dad and his wife to drive them to the Mayo Clinic in Rochester, Minnesota (only to do the reverse trip two days later), I heard this song by Casting Crowns. It communicates exactly the lesson I learned and the reason I continue to say, "I'm glad I didn't know."

Just Be Held

Hold it all together
Everybody needs you strong
But life hits you out of nowhere
And barely leaves you holding on

And when you're tired of fighting
Chained by your control
There's freedom in surrender
Lay it down and let it go

So when you're on your knees and answers seem so far away
You're not alone, stop holding on and just be held
Your world's not falling apart, it's falling into place
I'm on the throne, stop holding on and just be held
Just be held, just be held

If your eyes are on the storm
You'll wonder if I love you still
But if your eyes are on the cross

You'll know I always have and I always will

And not a tear is wasted
In time, you'll understand
I'm painting beauty with the ashes
Your life is in My hands

So when you're on your knees and answers seem so far away
You're not alone, stop holding on and just be held
Your world's not falling apart, it's falling into place
I'm on the throne, stop holding on and just be held
Just be held, just be held

Lift your hands, lift your eyes
In the storm is where you'll find Me
And where you are, I'll hold your heart
I'll hold your heart
Come to Me, find your rest
In the arms of the God who won't let go

So when you're on your knees and answers seem so far away
You're not alone, stop holding on and just be held
Your world's not falling apart, it's falling into place
I'm on the throne, stop holding on and just be held
(Stop holding on and just be held)
Just be held, just be held
Just be held, just be held.[3]

"'Honor your father and mother'—which is the first command-
ment with a promise—'so that it may go well with you and
that you may enjoy long life on the earth'" (Ephesians 6:2–3).

Questions to Consider

- Do you feel like you need to hold it all together and be strong for everyone? Consider the expectations you have placed on yourself or feel like others have placed on you and reflect again on the words above to "Just Be Held."

- If you are an aging parent, how can you help your children help you? Colossians 3:21 commands fathers to not exasperate their children. That is a great verse to consider in these situations.

- How can you give to meet the needs of your family but do so in a way that is encouraging to you and them and doesn't feel obligatory?

Painful Realizations

Name Withheld

This is a story in two parts. The first started when I was twelve years old. I was on a trip to New Orleans with my youth group when I took a nasty fall that triggered a rare nervous system disorder. The result was one of the most exhausting years of my life. From twelve to thirteen, I was in extreme pain (the disorder is quantified as greater pain than unmedicated childbirth or amputation of a finger). Thankfully, we were able to get a diagnosis right away and started working on a care plan. Because I was so young and my nervous system was still pretty pliable, there were ways for me to go into remission, although there was no cure for the disorder.

That entire year, I spent hours in physical therapy, followed by doing at-home exercises. I was on anti-seizure medications to help reset my nerves, though the medication always made me feel loopy and weird. I had a surgical procedure to try to rewire my nervous system. I was not allowed to run, jump, kick, or do anything that would impact my left lower leg. I always had to keep my leg warm, which meant wearing knee-high socks. Even in the summer. When I was twelve.

Thankfully, through God's great faithfulness and a mother who would not let me slack on any of my regimens, I successfully went into remission eleven months after my diagnosis. In my final appointment with my physician, I was warned that though I was in remission, any injury to my left side, especially my leg, could easily trigger a relapse.

For the next several years, I was always paranoid whenever I did anything physical. I was a competitive swimmer and engaged in all sorts of other teenage escapades, but there was always a small voice in the back of my mind warning me to be careful. I did not want to relive that year. As it always does, time carried on, and the voice became quieter as I continued to explore the world without injury.

Part two of this story picks up in the fall of my senior year of college. My time at university had been far from easy, but I had finally settled in, found my rhythms, found my people, and was living my best life. I had just started dating an amazing guy, was thriving in the three jobs I had at the time, and was thoroughly enjoying my capstone courses for my major. I would warrant to say it was the happiest I had been in a decade.

Of course, the sweetest of times rarely linger for long. The student group I was in leadership with, Cru (formerly called Campus Crusade for Christ), brought all the students in my state up to the mountains for a long weekend every October. It was one of my favorite parts of fall, and I was so excited for my last one. On the first night of these weekends, there was a massive dance competition between the schools. For the first time, my campus sent enough students for us to compete! We had been practicing, had put together some sweet costumes, and were ready to rock the dance floor. The week before, I had subluxed (minorly dislocated) my left knee. I was wearing a knee brace and gimping a bit but determined to go all out in the competition.

No one told my knee the plan.

I knew by the end of the night that I needed to go back on the crutches I had brought with me, "just in case." My knee had dislocated again, and I'd torn a couple of minor ligaments. The next day, I started getting scared. I could tell something was wrong with more than just my knee. The next twenty-four hours included a few frantic phone calls with my mother, lots of googling of the best doctors in the area, and a whole lot of fear. By the time I got back home from the weekend, I was certain—I had relapsed.

The "best" part was that I didn't just relapse with my left leg; this time, my entire left side, up to my face, was affected. I knew what was coming, and the anxiety was real. Pretty immediately, my world became all about the disorder again. I ended things with the guy I was seeing—there was no way I could handle a brand-new relationship on top of everything. I had to see multiple doctors and physical therapists and spent hours on the phone with my pharmacy, trying to figure everything out.

In the six weeks after the conference, I ended up having two more surgeries, with minimal relief. The bottom line was this: adults don't go into remission. Living with this disorder was going to be a reality for the rest of my life.

For the last four years, I have been living with it. I have also moved overseas, done lots of ministry, worked for amazing companies, and earned a master's degree. I am in no less pain today than I was four years ago, but I have found that our good Father provides the exact measure of grace to do the things He has called us to, pain disorders aside.

Glad I Didn't Know

Oh, how forever grateful I am that I had no clue going into my senior year that I was about to relapse. Had I known, I would not have made incredible friends; I would not have started a job that ended up being one of my favorite parts of the entire college experience; I would not have stepped out in faith to sign up to go overseas immediately following my graduation, and I would not have been happy. I got to have many months of happiness before the incident. If I had known, I would have spent too much time pre-grieving what was to come instead of living life to its fullest.

Lessons Learned

His ways are truly higher than ours. While I know the full purpose of my life and my suffering won't be revealed until I'm on the other side of Heaven, I am so grateful for the parts our good God decided to show me now.

Fear: I never realized how much fear I carried with the possibility of relapse until it all dissipated when it finally happened. As devastating as it was, there was such sweet relief knowing I no longer had to worry about bumping my leg anymore. I had let this fear occupy too much of my brain for far too long. Fear should never be a hallmark of believers, and I had unknowingly let it slip into my everyday rhythms. Being finally released from that fear made me aware that I had not been stewarding my anxieties well, and it put me on guard to notice them sooner moving forward.

Expendable crewman: One recurring theme throughout my health journeys has been the constant need to lay aside pride and the role I thought I should play in the Kingdom. I had always had these grandiose visions of what I could accomplish for God and was dedicated to building a resumé that would warrant the comment, "Well done, good and faithful servant," as it says in Matthew 25:23. My hero complex was challenged when my health worsened. Each day, I had very little capacity to do "great" things for God. My mom challenged me to live less like the hero and more like the expendable crewman—the one who does the little things that are crucial to the mission and does not seek or expect recognition for it. Saying a single prayer is still a great thing for God. It was surely an exhausting way to learn humility, but I am so much better off for it.

Witnessing: We always hear that actions speak louder than words, but I, at least, tend to forget that as I go about my day-to-day activities.

As believers, we are watched for how we act and react to struggles and successes. For a long time, I never thought that my suffering would serve real Kingdom purposes. However, our God is faithful, and throughout the years, He put people in my life who were not believers or who were struggling with faith. My pain sparked so many conversations with them about where my strength comes from and has built up the faith of many. How silly I was to assume the Lord couldn't or wouldn't use my life for His greater purposes.

Trust: When I relapsed, I didn't realize it at the time, but my trust in God was fractured. The word *trust* implies reliability. I did not feel as though the Lord was being reliable with my health; if anything, it felt as though He was being reckless. Kintsugi is a Japanese art form where broken pottery is repaired with gold, making it far more magnificent than before. It's the perfect metaphor for what happened with my trust in the Lord. Over time, this trust was rebuilt. I saw His immense care for me. I saw the purpose in (most of) my physical suffering. I was assured that God was being intentional in the road He was having me walk. My trust was restored tenfold, gilded in gold.

Suffering: It is what we're supposed to do. Not necessarily physical suffering and not necessarily all the time, but suffering produces righteousness, and that makes it a good thing. Just take a look anywhere in the Word, and you'll see how God uses suffering as a tool to refine us. Job was upright and blameless before the Lord, and in all his suffering, he "did not sin or charge God with wrong" (Job 1:22). Not only are we not to blame God, but we're supposed to rejoice in it. When we sign up for a life with God, we commit to carrying our crosses. My friends, that is not an empty promise we make.[4]

---

4   The author of this story has lived in many states across the US and multiple
     countries in Asia. She currently works as a public health researcher abroad while
     serving in local churches. Her name is withheld because of the sensitive areas
     where she serves.

"Consider it pure joy, my brothers and sisters, whenever you face trials of many kinds, because you know that the testing of your faith produces perseverance" (James 1:2–3).

Questions to Consider

- What lingering fear do you have that might be holding you back?

- What pain or discomfort are you experiencing now that seems like it may never go away (physical, emotional, or spiritual)?

- How has God restored a past pain to grow you to where you are today?

Faith Journey

While early childhood was maybe not idyllic, an important and foundational thing happened to me. My parents wanted what was best for me, and in their minds, that meant giving me the best education our small town offered. They found that in a Christian school only one block from our house.

The decision to do this was probably not easy. My family was proud to be of German heritage, and because of that, they were proud to be Lutheran, Missouri Synod Lutheran. Now, please understand: this topic is not here to disparage any specific denomination. The particular views of a denomination can take on a different form from one congregation to the next and have even changed over the decades since this story took place. I mention it because there were deep theological differences between the Lutheran Church and the Baptist Church, where this school was housed.

I loved the people at that school. I remember many of them fondly, and I felt a sense of peace and love there that became invaluable. However, I was only there for kindergarten through second grade. My parents' divorce resulted in my mom and I moving to a town about thirty miles away. There was no money for a private school. I missed it and begged to go to the Christian school that was in our new hometown.

Over the next few years, my mom remarried, and ultimately, she and her husband made the sacrificial decision to send all of us kids (his and hers) to the Berean Christian School, though we attended the Lutheran church in that town as well. The school was inexpensive by today's standards of tuition, but we had very little money, so I recognize this amazing gift. It was there I heard and saw the gospel lived out daily. I was taught the Scriptures and took part in chapel services and other activities where the Bible was explained and applied.

On November 30, 1987, I recognized my personal need for our Savior and accepted Christ into my life. I remember praying with a friend as we sat together on the steps by the ping-pong table. I recognized the eternal significance of that moment. This presented a new problem. What I came to believe didn't line up with what I was being taught in my family's church.

I sought a solution that would align what I learned during the week with what I learned on Sundays. Though a fourteen-year-old, I met with the pastor. I explained that I had come to understand the meaning of the Great Commission in Matthew 28, that you make disciples and then baptize them so there is a conscious decision to follow Christ (making disciples) that is critical to our eternal security. It wasn't infant baptism or any other act of the church that saved. He responded that a lot of the Bible is figurative. I determined that I wasn't smart enough to understand what was figurative and what was literal, so I would take the whole Bible with a literal understanding—that when it said something was "like" this or that, it was an illustration. I never attended that church again. My mom just wanted me to go to *a* church, so I went with my friends elsewhere from that day forward.

The town my mom lived near had a population of around 1,500, and the town my dad lived in had a population of 3,500. Those are small and, during this time in my life, they were small enough that the pastor of each of their churches was the same person. He spoke in one town, and when he finished, he drove to the other town and preached there as well.

My dad had custody of me every other weekend. We attended church together on the weekends I was with him, but on the other weekends, the pastor would report to him that I hadn't been in church. This had been going on for some time. One particular weekend, when I was sixteen, this topic came up while my dad and I were working outside. He was fairly adamant about which church I should be attending when I was at my mom's house. I tried as clearly as I could to explain what I believed and how I thought the differences were critically important. He, in essence, demanded that I give that up and return to the Lutheran church. I felt this was a test of my faith and that if I acquiesced, it would be admitting I didn't believe a personal relationship with Christ to be the sole means of salvation.

The conversation that day ended with my dad telling me that I needed to change my position or he would take me home to my mom's house. He was serious, and I packed my ever-faithful suitcase that went with me every other weekend and we drove the thirty miles in silence. When he dropped me off, he told me to call him when I changed my mind. We didn't speak for a year. By God's grace, Bryan and I were dating then—so I had his family, my teacher's family, and other friends who surrounded and encouraged me.

That was a defining moment for me . . . and such a painful time. The pastor even came to my mom and stepdad's home sometime later to meet with us and let me know I was formally excommunicated from their church. I can tell you that doesn't mean much to a sixteen-year-old, but it was just another indication of the stand I had taken, as well as another level of separation between my father and me.

Glad I Didn't Know

I'm glad I didn't know how the conversation with my dad would end. I'm afraid I might have backed down rather than stood up. I'm glad I didn't know the future family relationships that would be strained. My stepdad thought this was all ridiculous, and at one point, made life really difficult for his son who had also accepted Christ. My grandpa and grandma were disappointed, and they were two of the most important people in my life. We have a saying in our house: "The right thing is seldom the easy thing." That is so true!

Lessons Learned

I praise God that ultimately my parents and grandparents came to Christ. My dad mentioned later that part of his faith journey was the need to understand what was so important to me that I would be willing to risk our relationship. I sometimes wonder if I have grown complacent in my faith or would do the same thing if faced with a similar challenge today.

I am a huge proponent of Christian education. This was not only my anchor when the waves of life were tossing me to and fro, but also the lighthouse that ultimately pointed me safely into my Savior's arms. I believe it should be the best education you can get, and it should help believing youth grow in their faith and nonbelieving youth learn about what a relationship with Christ is all about.

I am extremely thankful for the influence of godly adults in the lives of children. My teacher and his family took me in and modeled a godly marriage and home, which has had a significant impact on the rest of my life. Bryan's parents were at church every time the doors were open, and as he joked, "They had a key, so they unlocked the doors when they weren't open." His mom served in the nursery and sang alto like an angel, and his dad had the wisdom of Solomon. It was recognized that he was a man of few words, but when he spoke, people listened. Since we dated while I was in high school, I had their influence during this important season as well. I love how others in our lives now have been that kind of influence on our girls. They have loved and listened to and encouraged and modeled godly behaviors when we, as parents, might have been dismissed.

Challenges to our faith grow us, and by their very name, they're not easy. I'm glad I didn't know what the challenges of my faith would result in, but I glory in the results the Lord produced from them.

> "Therefore, since we are surrounded by such a great cloud of witnesses, let us throw off everything that hinders and the sin that so easily entangles. And let us run with perseverance the race marked out for us" (Hebrews 12:1).

Questions to Consider

- What life steps did the Lord use to bring you to faith?

- Has standing up for your faith resulted in losses of any kind?

- What are you glad you didn't know would happen as a result of your faith journey?

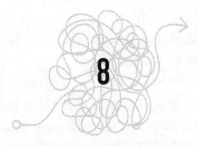

8

Do Not Be Afraid

James Ballard

M y wife, Rachél, and I loved college students. We led a ministry with World Gospel Mission at Asbury University. We lived on campus, invited the students into our lives, and quickly became the "campus mom and dad." It was because we fed them; once you start feeding college students, they come back! Rachél's heart for hospitality won over many students. It made them feel seen and welcome.

During the semesters at Asbury, we had a weekly service called Global Café, which focused on missions. On September 19, 2020, Rachél and I shared our story and testimony. Rachél used her favorite Bible passage from Isaiah 43:1–5:

> "But now, this is what the Lord says—he who created you, Jacob, he who formed you, Israel: 'Do not fear, for I have redeemed you; I have called you by name; you are mine. When you pass through the waters, I will be with you; and when

you pass through the rivers, they will not sweep over you. When you walk through the fire, you will not be burned; the flames will not set you ablaze.
'For I am the Lord your God, the Holy One of Israel, your Savior; I give Egypt for your ransom, Cush and Seba in your stead. Since you are precious and honored in my sight, and because I love you, I will give people in exchange for you, nations in exchange for your life. Do not be afraid, for I am with you . . .'"

Rachél shared that when she was six years old, she was run over by a car while she was riding her bike to school. The car's tire rolled over her head. She should not have survived. Throughout most of her adult life, she suffered from several autoimmune disorders that plagued her with pain and many questions but no answers. When she was thirty-five years old, about three years before we started serving at World Gospel Mission at Asbury, Rachél was diagnosed with breast cancer, and praise God that cancer was beaten. Through all of those moments, Rachél leaned into the reality that there was nothing to fear. She knew whose she was. She was called by name, and her God was with her, no matter the circumstances.

Fast-forward to late January 2021. Rachél developed headaches and nausea. She worked in health care as a nurse practitioner, so we thought she may have caught some virus, like COVID-19 or the flu. The headaches grew worse, and it seemed as if she was hearing sounds. I found her on the bathroom floor in terrible pain. We quickly rushed her to the emergency room where they did some tests. Covid was ruled out, so they decided to do scans of her head to see if there was any reason why she was having such severe headaches. When the neurologist came into the room to report on the scans, he said, "We found a mass on your brain, and we need to remove it immediately because it could be cancer."

We felt those words deeply. "It could be cancer." We had heard those words when Rachél was diagnosed with breast cancer six years before this moment. It felt like the floor was giving way beneath us. Our hearts and minds went in many directions. Rachél clung to Isaiah 43, "Do not fear, for I have redeemed you, I have called you by name, you are mine. . . . do not be afraid, I am with you." Worship music, prayer, and Scripture would fill the atmosphere of that emergency room while she waited for almost an entire week for surgery. In the waiting, you would find Rachél encouraging the young nurses and speaking life over them while they took care of her. This was juxtaposed with knowing if this was brain cancer, the only way she could find healing was if God would heal her. She lived in the reality of Isaiah 43, that no matter the circumstances, God was with her. She knew whose she was. She was His.

After surgery, on February 1, 2021, it was confirmed to be stage 4 glioblastoma, and it would be terminal, barring supernatural healing. She started chemotherapy and radiation treatments soon after her surgery. We hit the ground running because she wanted to be as proactive as possible. The tumor grew back after months of her enduring traditional treatments, like chemotherapy and radiation, and a newer treatment using electromagnetic therapy.

We had a phrase during the journey. "Our Hope is in the Healer, not the healing." No matter if God healed her in this life or the next, our hope was in the Person, not what He could do for us. He was our Hope, our Peace, our Joy. This was evident in how Rachél walked through this battle with cancer. Grounded in communion with God through His Word and prayer, Rachél was a beacon of hope and joy for those who were watching her in our community—and quite honestly around the world.

Living on a college campus, her journey with cancer was on full display at Asbury University. Students, faculty, and staff got a front-row seat for our journey. Rachél would meet with students as often as she could on our porch. She would speak of Jesus as if He was sitting right there on the porch with them. She would point students to the hope she had in

Him, no matter the circumstances, even as she battled terminal cancer. She never stopped pointing people to Jesus.

As the cancer progressed, it took away mobility and vision on her entire left side. She went from walking to using a walker, and eventually to being pushed in a wheelchair before she was put in hospice. As her body fought against her, she still pointed others to hope in Jesus. Here is what she wrote on Facebook on July 27, 2021:

> *Reading in Ephesians this morning, we are God's masterpiece, created to do good things, and He has a plan for each of our lives! I'm thankful He has a plan because I'd surely mess it up! Praise God for His great love for us! We can go to God our Father because He gave us His son Jesus who died for our sins, rose again, and gave us the gift of the Holy Spirit! Seek Him and you will find Him! God's presence has been palpable during our current struggles. He gives us the peace and strength we need to walk through the difficult times! Does this mean it's easy? No, but we can attest to God's great love and faithfulness! He is greater, stronger, [a] healer, and powerful! Trust in Him now! In this world, tomorrow is not guaranteed. We all need Jesus! Nothing can stand against us if God is for us! Thank you to everyone praying for us. God is answering and holding us up! With His strength we can live day to day and enjoy every moment. How can I pray for you today? —Rachél*
>
> "May God our Father and the Lord Jesus Christ give you grace and peace" (Ephesians 1:2, NLT)

She wrote this in her Bible during her journey: "I am a child of the King, the best is yet to come." Unbridled hope. She knew whose she was. She was His.

In the final week of her life, current students and former students filled our small living room where her hospice bed sat. Messages were sent through text messages, videos, emails, and phone calls from former students, friends, coworkers, family, and pretty much everyone who was touched by her life. Everyone told stories of how Rachél made them feel seen and how she showed them the depths of God's love for them. It was beautiful. I think we all got a glimpse of a holy moment, of a life well lived with Jesus. The presence and peace of God was palpable in the room. Rachél passed away on November 8, 2021. There was no fear. Just a daughter of the King being welcomed into the presence of her Hope, Jesus.

Glad I Didn't Know

I remember thinking, as I looked at Rachél fading in her hospice bed that last week of her life, that I would choose to marry her even knowing that I was going to lose her after twenty years of marriage. Now that I am years removed from her passing, I still would have said yes to marrying Rachél if I had known, but I am really glad I didn't know. We had twenty years together on this earth, years unfettered by the burden of that knowledge, and for that time we had, I am grateful and remain changed.

Lessons Learned

I will forever be marked by how Rachél faced brain cancer. I witnessed a faith, hope, and strength in Rachél that was breathtaking. During her suffering, Rachél's spirit never dimmed. Here's what I learned:

Hope in Suffering: So many times in my life, I have wanted to run away from hard, painful things. Rachél taught me through her journey that sometimes it's in the pain, the struggle, the hard, the desert, and the wilderness that we can find peace. We can find hope. It's in those times we learn in what or in whom we place our confidence and trust. If I am honest, many times I would place my confidence or faith in my circum-stances, so if it got hard, I often asked, "Where are you God?" That does not fit the character of Jesus, who endured suffering on the cross. God seems to do His best work in the wilderness, in the hard places, and yes, even in pain and suffering. Going back to Isaiah 43, he says in verse 19,

"See, I am doing a new thing! Now it springs up; do you not perceive it? I am making a way in the wilderness and streams in the wasteland."

Where is God doing a new thing? It is in the wilderness. It is in the wasteland. I have learned to embrace the struggle, the pain, and the hard because I know where my Hope resides, in the Person of Jesus, and sometimes those painful circumstances can point me directly to Him. I can thank Rachél for that example.

Gratitude: I love Colossians 3:15–17. It mentions gratitude or being thankful three times in that passage. I have learned that gratitude changes everything. It changes your posture with others and with God. Gratitude is more about expectancy than expectations, which means your hands and heart can receive whatever blessing is being given. Many times, we miss out on the blessings of loved ones because we are not grateful. We allow expectations to cloud our vision, and honestly, we close our hands and hearts to the blessings or gifts around us. When I am grateful, I have more peace, better relationships, a posture of worship, and a heart ready for action. I try to practice gratitude every day, thanking God by naming the gifts I have been given.[5]

---

5   James Ballard is a college pastor and mobilizer with World Gospel Mission at Asbury University in Wilmore, Kentucky. He is passionate about University of Kentucky basketball, barbecue, coffee, discipleship, cultivating culture, and empowering leaders. James and his late wife of twenty years have one biological son, Josh, and several hundred "adopted" children at Asbury University.

"Let the peace of Christ rule in your hearts, since as members of one body you were called to peace. And be thankful. Let the message of Christ dwell among you richly as you teach and admonish one another with all wisdom through psalms, hymns, and songs from the Spirit, singing to God with gratitude in your hearts. And whatever you do, whether in word or deed, do it all in the name of the Lord Jesus, giving thanks to God the Father through him" (1 Corinthians 3:15–17).

Questions to Consider

- "Our Hope is in the Healer, not the healing." If you were being honest, would you say you allow the circumstances of your life to dictate your hope? In what or whom does your hope truly rest?

- How do you practice gratitude? Have you told the people in your life that you are thankful for them?

- Are your hands and heart open with expectancy, not expectation of God and others?

A Piercing Question from Mother Teresa

Larry Probus

As a new Christian in the early 1990s, I read a biography about Mother Teresa's calling to serve the poorest of the poor in Kolkata, India (formerly Calcutta). She had sensed this call as a child, joining the Sisters of Loreto at eighteen and, soon thereafter, moving to Kolkata. Several years later, she experienced a "call within the call," to leave the convent to help the poorest of that city while living among them. I recall thinking that those who serve in the hardest places of the world as missionaries must have experienced similar callings and was glad God had not put that on my heart!

I was working for a publicly traded consumer products company at the time, and one of my corporate colleagues (and former boss) talked to me about his struggle with such a call. Rich Stearns was president of Lenox China when he was recruited to leave the corporate world to lead World Vision US as CEO. While joining World Vision entailed a move to Seattle rather than Senegal, it meant taking a big pay cut, turning in the keys to his corporate Jaguar, and uprooting his wife Renee and their five young children. Rich subsequently wrote about his fears and resistance to God's call in his book, *The Hole in Our Gospel*. "God was challenging me to decide what kind of disciple I was willing to be. . . . What was the most important thing in my life? He wanted to know. Was it my career, my financial security, my family, my stuff? Or was I committed to following Him regardless of the cost—no matter what?" Rich joined my wife Jan and me for dinner soon after he made the hard decision to join World Vision and shared his struggles of the soul. When he left, Jan asked, "Do you think we would ever do something like that ourselves?" We both laughed and said not likely.

About that same time, I began traveling to India to research consumer awareness and joint venture opportunities for the brands owned by the company for which I worked. It was the mid-1990s, and many of the US consumer product companies were investigating India and China for the first time, as both countries had recently opened their borders for trade. A colleague and I were checking out of a hotel in Kolkata, and the desk clerk overheard us talking about Mother Teresa. She told us if we wanted to visit "the Mother," we should tell our driver because everyone knew where she was located. Several hours before check-in for our flight home, we enthusiastically followed her suggestion.

We arrived at the Missionaries of Charity, an oasis in one of the poorest slums of Kolkata. Primarily ministering to perishing people seeking the opportunity to die with dignity, we were struck by the sacrificial servants working there. A sister asked us to wait until the Mother finished her prayers, and soon after, the Mother arrived and greeted us with the question, "Tell me why you are in my country." As a new Christian, the question was a piercing one. The specific reason for this trip was to establish a joint venture that would provide distribution for one of my company's whiskey brands. I contrasted this with Mother Teresa's reason for coming to India, and sheepishly responded with a very general, "We are here on business." After pondering this experience for a few hours, I said a silent prayer asking God to tell me if there was something He wanted with my life—other than peddling whiskey. With Rich Stearns's decision to serve marginalized children of the world as an example, I, too, wanted to be open to God's plan for my life.

Over the next several months, I explored some employment opportunities I thought would be more aligned with what God might want of me, including a chief financial officer position for an organization that served individuals with profound cognitive challenges. Doors did not open, however, and I found myself frustrated. After praying about this, I heard what seemed to be literal words from God in response: "You are where I want you to be. I've provided an excellent job that provides for your family. But hold loosely to these things because there is something else for you to do at a later time." That brought comforting closure to my troubling discussion with Mother Teresa, and I gladly accepted the promise that my current purpose in life was to continue working at a company with the many wonderful colleagues I had come to admire and respect.

Several years passed. Jan and I had four children. We were comfortable with friends, finances, schools, and nearby aging parents. My work was interesting, and I advanced beyond my expectations. Rich Stearns and I occasionally exchanged emails, and one day, he sent a *Washington CEO* magazine to us that featured his picture on the cover. The article told Rich's story of leaving corporate America to head World Vision's US operations, based in Seattle. After reading it, I put the magazine on Jan's mail stack, where it sat for several months.

One morning, I awoke to Jan telling me, "You are going to love what I prayed for you last night!" After going through unread mail when she couldn't sleep, Jan had read Rich's article and prayed that God would give us an opportunity to serve in the same way, and if that happened, that I would be willing. I smiled and said that would be nice and went to work.

Two days later, Rich called and said World Vision was looking for a chief financial officer, and my name had been on his heart. Could he give my contact information to the search firm? My reaction was, "Rich, the timing is not good to uproot my family. We have four young children and are taking care of Jan's mother who has Alzheimer's, but I will talk to Jan and get back to you." When I discussed it with Jan, she reminded me of the message God had given me several years before and encouraged me to participate in the interview process.

I found myself praying that God would bring someone much more qualified than me to World Vision. I knew nothing about the non-profit world of relief and development, and moving our family across the country to an expensive city while taking a hefty pay cut seemed overwhelming. *Maybe in five years, but not now.* At the end of the selection process, Rich called and said the World Vision team wanted to offer me the position.

Jan and I now had a decision to make. Like Rich's struggle years earlier, fears and apprehension caused us to delay. Did we really believe God was calling us to World Vision, or did the fact that Rich and I had worked together in the past just make me an easier choice than other candidates? Jan recalls me being downright angry with God for putting this choice on our plate.

After several weeks of prayer, soul searching, and seeking the wisdom of fellow believers, God spoke in an unexpected way. I was commuting to work, and a new billboard appeared on my daily route with a picture of Mother Teresa—and the words, "Reaching Beyond Yourself. Compassion. Pass it On." I called Jan and said, "I give up. I think God is telling us we should do this." God's message to me was, "Let go. I am in control; let me lead you."

I worked as the chief financial officer for World Vision US for thirteen years and now have the privilege of serving as a director of World Vision US, as well as on the World Vision International boards of directors. The transition for our family to the Seattle area could not have been smoother, and we have been so blessed to be part of World Vision's ministry. In particular, I count the experience of helping generous donors and other World Vision colleagues expand World Vision's clean water program (from 200,000 beneficiaries a year to nearly three million per year) as my life's greatest vocational achievement.

Glad I Didn't Know

I am thankful I did not know Mother Teresa would immediately engage me with the question, "Why are you here?" I assumed she would talk about her ministry and was not prepared for her probing inquiry about *me*. Had I known, I might have avoided the meeting and missed out on seeing the all-important juxtaposition of why we were each there.

Lessons Learned

During my first trip to India, I tried giving modest amounts of money to children on the streets but soon became overwhelmed with the need I saw and concluded there was nothing one person could do. The selfless work of Mother Teresa demonstrated one person, acting as a servant of the Lord, can indeed make a profound impact in a seemingly hopeless situation. This was a valuable lesson as I tried to understand the impact of World Vision's work in the hardest places in the world.

God is in control, and I am not. I see dimly what God sees clearly, and rather than set my own goals and objectives, I try to keep my heart open and tender to God's leading. It is often very different from my understanding! Having said that, I've also learned that God rarely shows us the complete picture of any future design. Instead, He tells us the next step to take.[6]

---

6   Larry Probus had a distinguished career in for-profit business, nonprofit, and higher education industries. He served on advisory committees to the Financial Accounting Standards Board and on the Standards Committee of the Evangelical Council for Financial Accountability. He currently serves on the board of directors for World Vision US and World Vision International.

"For now we see only a reflection as in a mirror; then we shall see face to face. Now I know in part; then shall I know fully, even as I am fully known" (1 Corinthians 13:12).

Questions to Consider

- Why are you here, wherever "here" may be?

- Are you doing what one person can do or waiting for the opportunity to make a "profound impact?"

- Is there a prompting or calling you are ignoring or delaying?

10

Not My Plan

I worked for a while after Bryan and I married and then went to college and completed a degree in accounting. I remember walking across the platform to get my diploma and holding it up to Bryan and mouthing the words, "We own it." We had worked hard for me to go through college debt-free, and now we could do anything.

We had no kids and decided we were ready for an adventure. We considered the possibilities of moving to New York, Seattle, or San Francisco, but the Lord had other plans.

During college, I worked at a Christian radio station. That station was owned by a ministry headquartered in Colorado Springs, Colorado. The general manager knew I wasn't going to keep working in radio with my accounting degree. He had the CFO of the ministry reach out to me. The CFO had connections with five public accounting firms in Colorado Springs. I sent my resume and received interviews with four of the firms.

Bryan and I had friends who had moved there the year before, so we drove down, and I blitzed through the four interviews in two days. The last of the four was with a firm called CapinCrouse. I left that interview and drove back to our friend's house. I told Bryan that I would turn down any offer to work with them. They only served churches and Christian ministries. I had never heard of such an opportunity.

As it turned out, I received an offer from another firm a couple of weeks later. CapinCrouse not only didn't have a position open (they interviewed me as a courtesy to the ministry CFO), but of the two people I met with, one had been moving out of state right after our interview and the other was on vacation, not to be disturbed. However, the managing partner called me from Indiana and interviewed me over the phone. By God's grace and the graciousness of the managing partner, they also extended an offer, and I had a choice about which firm to join.

While I was excited about this opportunity with CapinCrouse, I had my plans all laid out. I would pass the CPA exam, work at the firm for a couple of years to both get licensed as a CPA as well as get experience. After that, we would start a family, and I would leave the firm to work on my own, likely part-time. Let me guess . . . you've mapped out very specific plans before, too, and you're laughing right now at how I had it "all figured out."

A couple of years did find us welcoming our first child. I was allowed some flexibility in my schedule, and Bryan worked for a company that had a fantastic onsite daycare. Bethany was extremely social, and as she transitioned from an infant to a toddler, we found she preferred to be at daycare to home with me when I had the opportunity to work from home. I guess I'm rather boring compared to a room of toddlers and fun daycare workers.

Over the years, I was promoted from staff auditor to senior auditor. Then we made a family decision that led to Bryan staying home and me continuing to work. At that time, I progressed to manager and then to partner in this national firm. Ultimately, I served as a managing partner for a couple of years.

I didn't get to the end of the first two years and think, *I'm not going to stay home. I'm going to climb to the top. We're going to go from four offices to sixteen across the country, and I'll eventually be in a position of national leadership.* Hardly!

It was a series of decisions of varying significance. Sometimes the decisions were so small that I can't even recount them for you, and sometimes they were significant, such as deciding together that Bryan would stay home and I would work. All of these decisions were made over years, each one building on the last. Someone told me early on in my faith, "It's easier to steer a moving vehicle than one that is sitting still." That is so true. If you're sitting in a parked car, the steering wheel is really hard to turn, and you don't go anywhere. If you're driving down the road at 55 mph, the slightest adjustment to the steering wheel has you soon going in an entirely different direction. As I moved through my career, some small decisions here and there led to an entirely different result than I had ever fathomed in the beginning. This sheltered kid from South Dakota had the privilege of serving—and serving alongside some of the nonprofit world's leading experts.

Glad I Didn't Know

When I reflect on the path my career took during those twenty years, I'm glad I didn't know how it would turn out. You might ask, "Why?" because it seems like a pretty great career. It is! However, I realize that my personality is such that if I had known the result, I would have begun planning and positioning. I would have worked in my own strength to get to that end. Bottom line: I would have messed it all up.

Lessons Learned

It's only been in recent years that I have realized with my heart what we understand in our heads. That God's plans are so much better than ours. Really consider that for a moment. You probably agreed when you read that and thought it was an obvious statement to make, but do you clearly understand it? If God had only given me my plans, I would have missed out on so many amazing things. Thank you, Lord, for doing "immeasurably more than I can ask or imagine," as we are promised in Ephesians 3:20.

When you plan a trip, there are two possible purposes for that trip. First, you might plan to take a great vacation to an idyllic location. Maybe you will visit an all-inclusive resort or some globally famous destination, like Israel or New York City or Yellowstone National Park. Other times, you might take a trip all about the journey. It could be backpacking across Europe or driving cross-country or touring New England in the fall.

I thought I knew the destination, but what I really needed to focus on was the journey. That is how life should be for the believer also. Our destination is already secure. We know where we're going. We need to focus on the journey from here to there.

Sometimes it is the blessings of life that I'm glad I didn't know because the joy is in the journey, and I don't have to plot and plan every piece of that. I need to head in the right direction, follow the Spirit's leading, and see what amazing things I happen on along the way.

> "'For I know the plans I have for you,' declares the Lord, 'plans to prosper you and not to harm you, plans to give you hope and a future'" (Jeremiah 29:11).

Questions to Consider

- How have your life's plans changed?

- Can you see how God's plans were (or are) better than your plans?

- What would change if you focused on your journey instead of the destination?

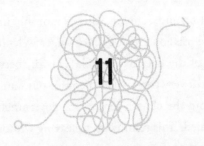

Hiding in Plain Sight

Marti Williams

My husband and I have served in leadership roles in our mission in three different countries (and on three different continents): Zimbabwe, United Arab Emirates, and Australia. Our experience has been one of transience and repeatedly reestablishing our life and ministry, and we have found some interesting—and even disappointing—strands of similarity in each setting, despite the reality of vastly different contexts.

We left for the mission field at the end of 1984 with our two-year-old daughter and plans for a church-planting career in Zimbabwe. While our responsibilities did include church planting, Ray was very quickly put into mission leadership positions. This turned out to be the start of a challenging career of navigating difficulties both in the mission and in the national church.

During our seven years in Zimbabwe, Ray was an integral part of negotiating the serious disagreements between the mission and the national church—the consequences of the "growing pains" of independence of both a nation and a church. This relationship finally broke down to the point where missionaries were no longer welcome to worship in the congregations of the national church. This rift between the mission and the church had a very personal element for our family. It came in the form of a letter from the church sent to the government requesting our family's visa be denied. This resulted in us leaving without knowing what our future held.

The next fifteen months were spent praying and asking our mission leadership where they felt we could minister, given our gifts and experience, but it remained unclear. In God's timing, we learned of another ministry area looking for administrative leadership, and Ray took a vision trip to see if this might be where God was leading. In May 1993, we nervously arrived in United Arab Emirates with three blonde, blue-eyed daughters, wondering how God was going to use us in this context. We had six years of fruitful ministry, and our daughters still view these years as some of the happiest of their lives.

In a few years, Ray began to discern some serious member care issues among our missionary personnel that needed to be addressed, and in his role as the ministry area leader, he sought the counsel of the Home Office leadership. They agreed with his assessment and gave him permission to encourage the local leadership team to take action. Unfortunately, this did not go as smoothly as hoped. Discouraged, we sought God's leading and followed His directive to "keep our counsel" and leave our reputation in His hands. Considering the circumstances, Ray felt he could no longer hold a position of leadership with the mission. We returned to the States, disappointed and discouraged.

Our mission director asked us not to leave the mission until he had a chance to get a few things approved. In due course, he offered us the opportunity to go to Australia to work alongside the Australian church in church planting and leadership development. Seeing God's leadership as a result of a vision trip in 1999, our family excitedly arrived in Australia in October 2000, and we all felt "at home" right away. We worked with a congregation to help them plant a church.

During our time of serving, though, there seemed to be unresolved issues hanging over our heads.

For the next few years, Ray and I served "under the radar" of our mission agency—under their auspices but with little connection. In 2008, we came on Home Assignment and had some painfully honest, but much-needed, conversations with our leadership. We were fully aware that we likely had made some mistakes, but leadership also owned the fact they had as well. That resulted in a restored relationship with the mission, and we returned to Australia to serve in various ministry roles until 2017. At that time, our visa was denied, and we had twenty-eight days to pack and leave the country we had faithfully served and come to love over nearly twenty years. This came disappointingly close to retirement, but we chose to trust God's timing.

Ray had already been put into an executive director position, in which he was responsible for the ministry of all missionaries in our mission around the globe. After our return to the States and some discussion with the new director, I was given a role in Equity and Diversity. These positions enabled us to prepare for our upcoming retirement while still ministering to the mission community. Part of that preparation has involved both of us becoming adjunct faculty at a Christian liberal arts college in our hometown. It was a blessing to be able to "finish well" and see the previous difficulties come full circle, to having the opportunity to invest in others and make an impact in a variety of ways within the organization where we had served for so many years. On March 31, 2022, we didn't retire, we redeployed!

Glad I Didn't Know

We left for the mission field a bit starry-eyed but not totally oblivious to the fact that interpersonal relationships are a major issue in that context. We are grateful for God's patience with His people. We learned firsthand the reality that sin doesn't just impact the sinner. There is always collateral damage, and it's painful! If we had known the difficulties ahead, we may never have said yes to the call God placed on our lives.

While we loved every country in which we lived and served, it was a *lot* of work, physically and emotionally, to liquidate everything and start all over again in each new context. Facing each of these moves one at a time rather than knowing about them all ahead of time was evidence of God's grace and love.

We also developed a sojourner's mindset as we learned firsthand what it means to be "just passing through" and keeping our eyes on our real home—with God our Father. Praise God there will be no suitcases and packing boxes in His presence!

Finally, we are so grateful that all the lessons God gave us to learn were spaced over time, and we didn't have to face them all at once. I am glad I didn't know any of them ahead of time!

Lessons Learned

The denied visas, which caused us to leave our place of ministry twice, were painful but not a surprise to God. In Zimbabwe, we learned our visa had been approved by all committees until the final person, who then denied it. In Australia, when we appealed our denied visa, it became apparent they thought we were trying to cheat the system, so we chose to withdraw our appeal to prevent dishonoring God's name.

Starting over again multiple times taught us to hold our "stuff" lightly. We have seen God provide our "daily bread" on a very daily basis! There was never much opportunity for stockpiling. When we see how He provided for our redeployment years, we are amazed and can only praise Him for our daily bread!

During the time when I felt "benched" in ministry, God led me to enroll in a study program, which later became the foundation for a women's ministry curriculum I wrote and taught in Australia—and am now teaching at Anderson University in South Carolina. This would not have happened if I had not had that "bench time" to invest in study.

While it took ten years, we sought to obey God and left our reputations in His hands. During this time, He "grew us up" in our faith in Him as we learned to desire His opinion of us over others. We learned to look at circumstances from God's perspective.

When we are in transition, our family often has a jigsaw puzzle going for those times when we can't sleep (for thinking about all we need to do). It helps us de-stress. Right after retirement (transition), we completed a 1,000-piece puzzle, only to find one piece missing. We searched everywhere—with no joy. To rub salt in the wound, there were two rogue pieces that didn't belong in the puzzle at all. Just before breaking the puzzle down, I sat back in my recliner and glanced at the puzzle again . . . and saw the missing piece on top of the puzzle, blending into the colors! Because of the coloring and our perspective (angle), we hadn't been able to see it. God, as the Creator/Source of the jigsaw that is our life, has provided all the pieces. God doesn't hide things from us. To find all the pieces to complete the picture, we need to see them all from His perspective, not our own. We also need to be aware that Satan, the great deceiver, is not above throwing in "rogue pieces" to distract and confuse us. Consistently looking at our lives from God's perspective enables us to complete the picture God is creating in and through us.

Leaving Australia where we were well-known and often called on to minister in different settings, it was difficult to settle in the town where God led us to retire—where no one even knew our names. We are humbled and grateful for how God has opened doors for us to continue in ministry and use our training and experience to prepare the next generation.[7]

---

7   Marti Williams grew up in South Africa and served with her husband, Ray, in
    missions for thirty-seven years. She focused on the areas of church planting,
    leadership development, women's ministry, and equity and diversity. Marti is now
    "redeployed" and is ministering in her local congregation and as adjunct faculty at
    Anderson University, in Anderson, South Carolina.

"Since my youth, God, you have taught me, and to this day I declare your marvelous deeds. Even when I am old and gray, do not forsake me, my God, till I declare your power to the next generation, your mighty acts to all who are to come" (Psalm 71:17–18).

Questions to Consider:

- How do you respond when you sense the difficulty you are experiencing may be because of someone else?

- How do you go about finding God's perspective of your life's puzzle when it appears some pieces are missing?

- What types of losses are the most difficult for you to work through (financial, relationship, reputation, status, etc.)? Why do you think that is?

12

Going to America—Really!

Dr. John Reynolds

W hat young girl or boy raised in the remote copper mines of Northern Rhodesia (now Zambia) did not hear stories of wonder and
amazement for those lucky enough to live in America? Comic
books like "Richie Rich," motor cars called Cadillacs, a television in every
home, sports celebrities like Muhammed Ali, musicians like Bob Dylan,
and a country that sent men to walk on the moon amplified the wonders
of the amazing country, the United States of America. Heads of young
people were filled with the seemingly "impossible" dream of going to live
in America.

Several moves in southern Africa—with the associated change in
schools and friends, as my father looked for work—and the reality of
growing up caused this dream to fade. However, that was BJ (before
Jesus). In a series of events during my last years of high school, I came
to faith, a decision that changed—as God does—an ordinary life into an
extraordinary life, to serve Him and His purposes.

Like many testimonies, it did not start well, with a failed first year in university, broken family relationships (being a first-generation Christian is not easy), and a lot of questions to my newfound Lord. Today, as a university leader, we would name this a "first-generation" context, but as God does, He was redirecting me to my future through studies in a then-new field: computer science. This was an important pivot in my life story as this new field would frame my career in mining, non-governmental organizations (NGOs), and higher education for the next forty-plus years. It was also the trigger to a series of events that, at age twenty-four and newly married, I landed with my wife in America to serve with an international NGO. The dream had come true, and we had arrived. How impressed our family and friends were that we had accomplished the "impossible" dream—moving to America!

As with many life stories, though, God had different plans. In less than two years, and pregnant with our first child, the dream slowly turned into a mirage, and we were back in South Africa. On the positive side, the goal was accomplished, and we had an adventure that few in our community had ever experienced. However, as God often does—and I am so glad I didn't know, but we'll get to that—He had other plans for us. God wastes no one and no experience!

Over a period of seven years (doesn't that sound biblical?), our world changed again. Checklist for life at the time: two great kids—done! Traveled around the world—done! Executive position in one of the largest mining companies in the world—done! Super house with a pool in a major city—done! Luxury German motor vehicle—done! Amazing church—done! Great community of family and friends—done! Graduate degree—done! As the famous Gershwin lyrics state, "Who could ask for anything more?" Then, driving one afternoon to visit family, with my six-year-old son in the passenger seat, we stopped at a traffic light. With a macho roar, a sporty new Porsche convertible pulled up next to us.

"Is that your next company car, Dad?" came the question from my young son's mouth.

Inside, I heard God's question: "Is this what I have called you to in serving me?" A deep time of prayer and reflection followed, leading to another major change in my life, and of course the life of my family. It started when I received a communication from the vice president for Africa of the global NGO where I had previously worked. The visit from this leader resulted in an invitation to join his executive team in Africa, which would require a move to Harare, Zimbabwe, and this invitation started a sequence of events peppered with moments changing my, and my family's, trajectory forever.

Resignation (much to my non-believing family's shock) from an excellent job at a top company, selling a wonderful home, searching for an international school in Harare for my son (the "Porsche" messenger from God), a transition to a new country, and a very different role were the starts to this new adventure. Just a few weeks before the big move, late at night, the telephone rang. It was my hiring VP, sharing he had just resigned that day, and the position he had offered me was rescinded; everything was now off.

As one would imagine, the next few days were a blur and full of questioning. Do I ask for my old job back? How do we find another home? What is God teaching us? I now had an ecstatic family, hoping we'd stay in South Africa! Then another late-night call came, this time from my previous supervisor at the NGO, sharing his disappointment that I would not be serving in Africa, but he had a new proposition. If I could move myself and my family over to California, USA, in the next sixty days (through our own means), he would hold a position for me and assist in obtaining a work visa. After prayers, tears, and confusion, we made the decision to use our savings and move for two years for me to lead this global project and then return to South Africa and regroup for the future.

On a hot summer Saturday in July 1991, we arrived in Los Angeles, and I started work that following Monday. A week later, we found a condo to rent and with our last dollars, we purchased a six-year-old car for my wife to use for the family. The local public bus became my "company car," and we lived using only the cash we had on hand, down to the penny. Newsflash for new immigrants; no credit history, no assets . . . no credit cards! Just a few months removed from living the "large life" in South Africa, I was traveling on buses, budgeting with envelopes, and living in a rented condo. If we had only known! Was this really the American dream I had envisioned growing up? Was this really the land of unlimited opportunity?

I am so glad we "burned the boats" in leaving our home country because life seemed so good there. Were we now parroting the Hebrews in the desert, saying to Moses, "Why is the Lord bringing us into this land, to fall by the sword? Our wives and our little ones will become a prey. Would it not be better for us to go back to Egypt?" (Numbers 14:3, ESV).

Glad I Didn't Know

God's plan is so much better than our plan! In this second phase of our lives in the USA, now spanning over thirty years, we have enjoyed a time of personal growth, lots of adventure, and much joy. We've gained two American daughters; I've received a post-graduate education and enjoyed several new and challenging careers. The unexpected NGO position offered in 1991 helped me grow professionally and shaped who I am as a leader today. The move affirmed my love for the "whole world" and my passion to equip, encourage, and grow Christian leaders to their God-given potential. It opened up the opportunity to switch careers from NGOs to Christian higher education and experience the impact Christ-centered colleges and universities have on young people's lives to go out and make a difference for Jesus in the world. It has included the honor of my two sons meeting two amazing women of God. It also provided the opportunity and space to meet Christian leaders in ministry, higher education, and the business world who have influenced me forever, as well as to be part of the global Church in spreading the gospel, serving, and, where possible, equipping.

Would I have enjoyed God's purpose and plans for my life if I had known? Would I have had the same experiences and become who I am today by staying in the comfort of what I knew? The answer must be a resounding no! "'For I know the plans I have for you,' declares the LORD, 'plans to prosper you and not to harm you, plans to give you hope and a future'" (Jeremiah 29:11). May it be so for you!

Lessons Learned

There is a significant gap in my understanding between believing and faith. Most believers, I am sure, learned this sooner than I did. I absolutely believed that God was sovereign in my life; I believed in His promises to give me the desires of my heart; I believed in His promises, and I believed He would always provide. However, as James 2:19 reminds us, "You believe that there is one God. Good! Even the demons believe that—and shudder." If I had known how difficult this transition was going to be for my family, would I have done it? Probably not, but the conviction of surrendering and obeying God, trusting God in the consequences, was a first step in my journey of faith. I certainly want to believe in all I read, but I especially want to experience God in His fullness and surrender unconditionally in faith.

God's journey for us is for our good and always for His purposes if He leads like it says in Romans 8:28. The story of the Exodus shares that God led His people on the long road through the desert on their journey to the Red Sea. I wonder how I might have felt after hundreds of years in slavery, living through the plagues, witnessing the Passover, and fleeing the Egyptians, who were hard on my heels, if I knew God was taking the "scenic" route. Then God showed up with a better plan. He went ahead of them in a pillar of cloud by day and a pillar of fire at night, it says in Exodus 13.

My journey—and yours—with God is unique. It does not and should not replicate or mirror any other believer's journey. I was specifically chosen. "You did not choose me, but I chose you and appointed you so that you might go and bear fruit—fruit that will last" (John 15:16a), before the foundation of the world (Eph 1:4), while in my mother's womb (Jeremiah 1:5), to be His chosen one for this journey in life.[8]

> "Being confident of this, that He who began a good work in you will bring it to completion until the day of Christ Jesus" (Philippians 1:6).

Questions to Consider

- What comforts might you wrestle to give up if called to do so?

- When has someone asked you a question that stopped you immediately, much like, "Is that your next company car, Dad?" did for me?

- Are you experiencing a gap between believing and your faith?

---

8   Dr. John Reynolds has served in a variety of executive roles, including being named the first president of Los Angeles Pacific University. He has vast experience on boards of directors, serving on multiple national and international nonprofit and corporate boards concurrently. John writes frequently on leadership, strategy, and board governance and has a strong desire to pour into others while being a lifelong learner himself.

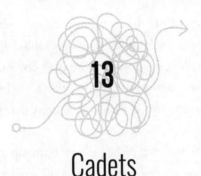

13

Cadets

I n 2001, while living in Colorado Springs, I learned of a program at the United States Air Force Academy where families in the community could "sponsor" a cadet. This allows cadets to get off of the base and be "normal" college-aged kids for an evening or a weekend. We really enjoyed attending Air Force football and basketball games, and we were incredibly impressed with the young men and women there. We had been on many college campuses and had never seen such respectful and pleasant students. We wanted to support that environment.

I began inquiring about the qualifications and the requirements. Neither Bryan nor I have served in the military or come from military families. That would typically put us at a disadvantage to participate, but that year in particular, there was a shortage of families, and we were approved.

In July, the Academy had a special day where families met their sponsored cadets and took them home for the day. Think of it as a test drive for both the cadet and the family. We were excited and yet a little nervous. We were parents to a two-year-old daughter. We had been assigned a young man from Florida. What did we know about teenage boys?

A couple of days before the event, we received a phone call; because of the shortage of sponsor families, they were asking approved sponsors if they would be willing to sponsor more than one cadet. Two teenage boys?! We felt in over our heads. Yet, we didn't feel like we should say no to this opportunity, and if there was a need that we could fill, we should help.

The day came, and we picked them both up on the Academy grounds. The freshman class was about 1,000 students, broken down into forty-one squadrons. These two guys didn't even know each other because they were in different squadrons. As we drove home, everyone started to get acquainted.

The boys shared stories of their short time so far at the Academy. Neither of them came from military families either, so this was a significant adjustment. At that time, freshmen (Plebes) were not allowed to have cell phones, and neither freshmen nor sophomores could have cars. They were disconnected from the outside world. They could share their challenges, frustrations, and observations with each other in ways they certainly couldn't have with us.

My rule that day and each day forward was this: the first thing you do when you get to our house is call home. Your family needs to hear from you. They did that, and then we ate and just let them hang out and relax. It was a great day and the start of a journey that has continued for over twenty years.

You may be able to put the timeframe together and see that this was the summer of 2001. In just a couple of months, the United States would experience an event that would change some aspects of life permanently. September 11 is a day none of us who were alive will forget. Keep in mind the Air Force Academy is an active military base. The restrictions that had been in place before were nothing compared to what was put in place to protect the young men and women who were part of the Academy in the weeks and months that followed 9/11.

We were not allowed on the base to pick up our sponsored cadets. As the situation stabilized, leadership at the Academy recognized the need for the cadets to get off the Academy grounds. They bused the cadets to a local mall. We were notified of the day and time to pick them up there. Previously, they were always required to be in their uniforms when off the base, but the new threats changed that, and they were not allowed to wear their uniforms when they left the Academy because they might be seen as targets. It was actually comical to be at the mall and look around. You could easily identify every cadet in there. The age and hairstyle were a complete giveaway. They may have been in civilian clothes, but everyone knew who they were.

I can't imagine how concerning this must have been for their parents. The US had been in a state of peace for decades, and there had never been a widespread terrorist attack within our borders. Now these families with no military experience knew their children were not only potentially going to defend our country, but they could be targets of what were virtually unknown terrorists. It became more important that the boys called home first thing when we picked them up during those days.

Time passed, and they became a special part of our family. The guys were so good with our daughter. Their families would come for Parents' Weekend on campus, and we always had a big get-together. The stories we have will give us laughs for a lifetime. We shared good times and bad times during those years. The guys even came to the hospital to visit me when I was there for a month during my pregnancy with our youngest daughter. I'm so impressed with the thoughtfulness of two young men taking time from their crazy Academy schedules to just hang out and let us know they cared.

We went on to sponsor four cadets, two of whom were brothers. We have stayed in contact with three of them, been to three weddings, enjoyed getting to see four of their children, gone out of our way to see each other in various parts of the country, and just generally continue to care. I'm so proud of the men and women they have become and so thankful to have been a part of their lives.

Glad I Didn't Know

I'm glad I didn't know that this simple introduction to a teenage boy by a young couple with a toddler would last a lifetime and grow to include numerous other people. "Why?" you might ask. Because the planner in me would have wanted to make sure it was the perfect match. I would have been nervous about making the right impression on the kids and their families. It would have been more like a marriage if it was going to be for decades.

The fact is that it was a simple decision at a point in time when we wanted to invest in a culture and a student body to offer encouragement and support. The Lord did the rest. I didn't have to do anything but fill out an application and pass some background checks.

Lessons Learned

You never know who the Lord will put in your life and how long the impact will last. We had the opportunity to share Christ with these men, not by using a tract or requiring they attend church with us but by sharing our house, our food, our TV, and our care. That's all we're asked to do . . . is to be available and love one another.

> "Do nothing out of selfish ambition or vain conceit. Rather, in humility value others above yourselves" (Philippians 2:3).

Questions to Consider

- Who do you have in your life now that you never anticipated when the relationship first started?

- Is there an opportunity for you to open your heart and invest in someone now?

- Are there areas in your life where you are operating out of selfish ambition rather than being willing to give of your time, skills, or finances?

14

God Will Never . . .

Stan Reiff

A my and I met as high school seniors and dated through college at a small Bible college. Amy pursued a degree in elementary education, and I pursued Bible Studies, Pastoral Ministries, and Missionary Aviation majors with a plan to return to Latin America as a church-planting missionary pilot family.

As our relationship got more serious and we were discussing our potential future together, Amy asked a couple of insightful questions. Her first question was . . .

How do you know God's will for your life?

I shared with Amy that I felt confident in God's calling on my life based on the following factors: I was the third generation of a missionary family, born in Latin America. Spanish was my first language, and I had only recently moved to the USA for high school and college. I felt more

Hispanic than American, and for me, going back to Latin America was like going home to the family business. I told Amy I felt like it would be a waste of my upbringing and heritage to live in the US, and it certainly would not make sense for us to live in the north with cold weather, snow, ice, and limited, if any, Spanish speakers or Hispanic communities—you know, like God would never call us to, umm, *Alaska.* Yeah, God would never do that.

Amy's second insightful question also had a lasting impact on us.

Do you think God would ever give us a child with disabilities?

You see, Amy has an older sister who lives with cerebral palsy as a result of complications at birth that left her without enough oxygen for about twenty minutes. Amy grew up living with and helping care for Cathy. This was an important question for Amy as she contemplated the life of a missionary wife and mother in a remote jungle setting.

As the young, confident theologian, I responded that I was deeply compassionate and caring for those who lived with disabilities and chronic illnesses, but I was confident God would not give us a child with disabilities because it was inconsistent with God's call on our lives to be a remote, church-planting, missionary pilot family in the jungles of Central or South America. I was so confident of this that I actually told Amy, "I don't think God would allow that because it would impede our ability to fulfil His calling and would limit our ministry, if not make it impossible."

Fast-forward a couple of years and Amy and I found ourselves moving to . . . of all places? Yeah, you guessed it. We packed up our belongings and drove to North Pole, Alaska, where we served as missionaries for seven years.

We had just settled into our new work; Amy and I were teaching at the mission school in Fairbanks and also helping lead the youth group in a church in North Pole. Together with our close friends from college, Don and Kathy Irvine, we co-founded a flying ministry to fly missionaries, youth groups, and evangelists in and out of remote Alaskan villages. We were wrapping up our first year in North Pole, acclimating to our new environment while making plans to move into the remote fly-in village of Tetlin, an Alaska Native Indian community in the interior of Alaska. Amy was pregnant, and we were excited for our firstborn to arrive in June, shortly after the school year ended.

Amy ended up having complications with her pregnancy, and before we knew it, Stanley Jr. was born two months premature on April 4. He spent eight weeks in the NICU in Fairbanks. Our first couple of weeks were traumatic as he fought for his life. We were finally able to bring him home on Memorial Day weekend. But it was not long before we started dealing with new challenges. Because of his preemie status, Stanley was incredibly irritable. It seemed like he cried thirty hours a day, ten days a week. In June, the doctors confirmed he needed surgery to remove the top portion of his skull because the soft spot had already fused, increasing the pressure on his brain as it tried to grow. In September, we flew to Children's Hospital in Seattle to have this corrective surgery.

A few weeks after we returned home from Seattle, Stanley was diagnosed with cortical visual impairment. Two or three weeks later, Stanley was also diagnosed with cerebral palsy (CP). By the end of the first year, we were forced to acknowledge that Stanley had experienced severe and profound disabilities and was medically complex. To summarize, Stanley experiences CP, is visually impaired, is non-verbal, and has a seizure disorder. Stanley requires care 24/7.

As the reality of Stanley's condition set in, we were also faced with the crushing financial impact as we accrued almost a million dollars of medical expenses by the end of Stanley's first year. I could not travel to raise our support, and we realized we would not be moving to Tetlin. It was a devastating season for us.

I reflected on the two questions Amy had asked while we were dating and pondering marriage. I did not feel the same confidence of that "brilliant nineteen-year-old theologian." I had been wrong on both accounts regarding God's will. Amy and I were not living in the Amazon with a healthy son. Instead, we were stranded in North Pole with our firstborn, who needed to be near a major hospital because of his medically complex condition—oh, and we were financially broke.

Amy and I struggled to keep our lives together as we fought all of the emotions of our collapsed dreams, which had transpired within a few months. Disappointment set in as we faced the emotional, physical, psychological, financial, and spiritual battles. I watched my dream of being a church-planting missionary pilot vanish, not just from the tropical jungles but from the frozen tundra of Alaska too.

I was forced to find a job with a salary and benefits. I found an accounting position at the State of Alaska's Department of Fish and Game, which provided desperately needed family health insurance. It was God's graciousness and provision that paid for me to earn my MBA. I continued to be bi-vocationally involved with our church in North Pole and with our flying ministry, but my heart ached to be back in full-time ministry. My mind kept wandering back to my strong views that having a child with disabilities would impede my ability to have this ministry. Maybe even limit or prevent me from ministry at all. I was watching it all play out.

At age five, Stanley had to have both hips rebuilt. Winters with fifty-below-zero temperatures (or more) were really hard on him as he sat in his metal wheelchair, with bolts, plates, and screws in both hips. We realized we had to move.

In 1994, God brought us an opportunity to move to Kodiak, Alaska, where I was hired to be the Director of Finance and the Director of Development. This allowed us to be back in vocational ministry. The mission provided everything we needed to meet Stanley's needs: a full-time salary, health insurance, and a much warmer climate.

In 1999, Stanley was experiencing additional educational and medical needs that could not be met on Kodiak Island. We needed to relocate again. Because of Stanley's disabilities, we explored where we could move so that he'd have his medical and educational needs met.

The year 2000 found us moving to Atlanta, Georgia, to work for John Maxwell's non-profit, EQUIP. In late summer of 2001, Stanley received his much-needed surgery—a baclofen pump implanted into his abdominal cavity. A few weeks later, September 11, marked all of our lives forever. Even though Amy and I considered the possibility of moving back to the safety of the Alaska we knew, Stanley's surgery a few weeks earlier prevented us from returning because the regular maintenance and the refilling of the pump were not medical services available in Alaska at that time.

In January 2002, I had the opportunity to join the executive team at Crown Financial Ministries, where I was mentored by Larry Burkett and Howard Dayton. I had discovered Larry Burkett on the radio right after Stanley's birth when we were facing an impossible mountain of financial medical obligations. Larry's ministry had positively impacted our lives at a desperate time. I still pinch myself that I was able to serve on this ministry team for over a decade.

Stanley aged out of school at twenty-two, about the same time I transitioned from Crown and started a consulting practice to work with ministries and churches. God was again gracious and provided clients, and I experienced rapid growth. However, as I approached my first-year anniversary as a small business owner, I realized I was not going to be able to grow fast enough to secure group health insurance before my COBRA insurance expired. I was racing against the clock. I needed to have group health insurance for Stanley's ongoing medical care, and that was not something I could risk. I started looking at some acquisition opportunities, but nothing worked out.

In the fall of 2011, CapinCrouse approached me about joining the firm to head up their consulting division. I had been a raving fan of the firm as a client for the previous decade. I was grateful for the opportunity to be a part of the organization, which provided me with the family health insurance we needed for Stanley while also allowing me to continue to serve in God's Kingdom.

Glad I Didn't Know

As I reflect on our marriage and journey, I am so glad Amy and I did not know what was ahead. The seven years in North Pole were filled with gut-wrenching challenges, but it formed our character. And yes, even as I reflect on my old views that God would *never* send us to Alaska as missionaries, I realize they are now some of the most tender memories in our lives—the place our three sons were born and where our faith was tested.

Lessons Learned

Has having a child with special needs impeded our ministry? Absolutely not! Stanley has been the catalyst for all of our ministry decisions and opportunities. It has been because God placed Stanley in our lives, that He has directed each move. From pivoting to bi-vocational ministry and working at the Alaska Department of Fish & Game to earning my MBA as the foundation to becoming a CPA, from moving to Kodiak Island for a warmer climate required for Stanley's health to our relocation to Atlanta for him to get this much-needed pump surgically implanted, and to my ten years at Crown followed by now over a decade at CapinCrouse, we have been cared for, blessed, and divinely appointed to fulfill the purposes for which God intended. These transitions have all been through the filter and lens of Stanley's needs.

I would have been content to live in a remote Latin American jungle, the frozen tundra of North Pole, or the isolation of Kodiak Island, but because we put Stanley's needs first, God allowed us to have incredible opportunities to serve in and with organizations having a transformative impact on His Kingdom around the world. Thank you, Stanley, for being the special person God has used to lead our family in ministry these past thirty-five-plus years.[9]

> "Where shall I go from Your Spirit? Where can I flee from your presence? If I go up to the heavens, you are there; if I make my bed in the depths, you are there. If I rise on the wings of the dawn, if I settle on the far side of the sea, even there Your hand will guide me, Your right hand will hold me fast" (Psalm 139:7–10).

Questions to Consider

- How do these verses make you think about God's sovereignty in your life?

- Have you ever been disappointed with where God placed you? How did you respond?

- Why are stories of faith despite hardship so inspiring? Why don't we assume their faith was misplaced?

---

9   Stan Reiff's professional experience includes over thirty-five years in ministry operations, public accounting, government accounting, and international missions. Stan has been married to Amy for forty years, and they have three adult sons, two daughters-in-law, and three grandchildren. They are committed to building strong relationships and creating a family legacy that endures over time.

Gone Too Soon

The year 1998 was exciting. We bought our first home, we attended the MLB Home Run Derby in Denver, and our first daughter was born in October. Though, within a few weeks of her birth, we learned of my brother-in-law's cancer diagnosis. We couldn't fully comprehend what lay ahead.

Wayne was diagnosed with melanoma. Honestly, skin cancer didn't seem that concerning to me. We had no idea it was one of the mostly deadly cancers at the time. It is not typically the skin cancer that kills. Rather, it metastasizes somewhere else and can be very aggressive.

Bryan and Wayne were really close. There was a nine-year age difference between them. While Bryan was the younger brother, Wayne was the big kid. I'm not kidding when I say he was a big kid because he was six-foot, nine—eighty-one inches of total goofball.

Wayne was also competitive with every bone in his body. I have the same sense of competition, and he and I loved to compete with each other. Anything we did became a challenge. One of the few times I saw him genuinely frustrated was when I beat him at bowling. I still remember that fondly! Another competition memory involves the four of us leaving a restaurant. I thought, *I know he and I are going to end up racing. His legs are as long as my body. If I take off first, I'll have a little advantage. Then, when he starts to pass me, I'll push him. That will give me the element of surprise, and I might have a chance to win.*

It started off just as I had planned. I heard him coming, and at the time I determined to be perfect, I gave him a big shove. Let's put it this way; I'm an accountant and obviously not very good at physics. My mass pushing on his mass only made me lose *my* balance and trip over my feet, resulting in *me* going to the ground and completing about three full flips. Wayne, the ever competitor, finished running to the vehicle for the win and *then* came back to see if I was still alive.

That competitive spirit may also be why the cancer diagnosis didn't faze me at the beginning. I knew he would see this as another challenge and face it head on. He wasn't about to lose. There might be some obstacles but certainly nothing he couldn't overcome.

At the time Wayne began treatments, he was divorced and the single dad of three school-aged kids. He was an electrician with a demanding job. He didn't have a strong support system nearby. We wished we could be more available to him, but we lived in Colorado, while he lived in California, and Bryan and I both had jobs. As the treatments progressed, they took their toll on Wayne physically and emotionally. Thankfully, Bryan was able to go out a couple of times, just to lift his spirits. Those were some great memories even though they were the result of a difficult situation.

Then came the spring of 2000. Tests confirmed the cancer had moved to his brain and not in a small, operable way. It had taken over. Wayne searched for options and even flew to Houston to be treated by specialists at MD Anderson. This was another opportunity for the guys to be together, and Bryan flew there so they could hang out between appointments. The most memorable part of the trip was a ridiculous steak dinner and a day at Six Flags amusement park. There was one ride that Wayne really wanted to go on, but he was a little too tall. It wouldn't latch, but Bryan decided if his brother wanted to go, it was going to happen. He used all of the strength in his six-foot-five body and forced the harness down into the latch. He knew Wayne would love the ride, and they'd figure out how to get him out later!

Unfortunately, nothing would stop this vicious disease. He continued to decline. The cancer caused mini-seizures, and periodically, his talking would become incoherent. He needed more day-to-day care. Bryan and I took turns flying from Colorado to California one week at a time. Our daughter, Bethany, was not quite two, and one time, when I told her we were going to the airport, she said, "To see Daddy?" She thought that was where he was living because that was where we kept meeting. Wayne's best friends had just moved back from England, and they played an enormous role in his care too. His friends quickly became our friends.

By September, he was tripping periodically and required someone to pay attention to him around the clock. We didn't want him wandering or falling. The physical and emotional wear was taking its toll. One day, we took Wayne to a doctor's appointment. Wayne, the competitive optimist, asked what else could be done. The doctor referred to a new trial that was untested and that would be very difficult on him physically, with no indication of what the outcome might be. Wayne wanted to try it, and the doctor said he would check into it for him.

I asked Bryan to take Wayne to the check-out desk. Our friend and I cornered the doctor in the exam room—literally. I wanted to know if this was a real option. The doctor said no. He just didn't want to take hope away from Wayne. We told the doctor we had been told we couldn't get hospice help until a doctor said he likely had twelve months or less to live. Did he think we were there so we could get help? He immediately answered, "Oh, I think he has about thirty days left." He didn't have the courage to tell Wayne this himself, and we were forced, as his family and friends, to do so that afternoon.

The search began for hospice help. Our friend and I interviewed potential caregivers. I'm not sure what the agency was thinking, but it was good there were two of us involved in the process. If there had only been one of us, we might have done something we regretted. As it was, we could keep each other calm and usually ended up laughing, almost hysterically. For example, they sent one person over who was about five feet tall and one hundred pounds. It was obvious; there was no way she could meet the physical demands of the job. Then we had a lady who was about six feet tall and 200 pounds. She was perfect. She said she would only do it if her aunt was hired as well. She was the same size. Even better! However, when we discussed the duties, they made it clear they didn't do any lifting! Another name to cross off the list. Just when we thought we'd lose our minds, a nurse recommended two angels. They were available, and they were amazing. This allowed us to spend the last couple of weeks simply being with Wayne, the kids, and each other.

On October 7, 2000, we lost a brother, a best friend, a competitor, as well as a big piece of our hearts. We knew he wasn't suffering anymore, but we were. He made it clear he had a personal relationship with Christ, and we appreciate that we will see him again someday. We were all hurting but thankful that he was done with the battle.

Glad I Didn't Know

I was twenty-five when this journey began. I'm glad I didn't know we would see the beginning of our precious daughter's life and the end of life with our beloved brother in the same season. It would have been overwhelming to know we would have to navigate the medical system and provide home care while nurturing a young child. I would have freaked out if, as new parents, I knew we would have to provide an environment for a high schooler, a middle schooler, and an elementary child to treasure their dad's last days while their friends went on with life as usual. I'm glad I didn't know that planning a funeral is like planning a wedding in four days, from the invitations to the flowers, and from the food to all of the other details. I couldn't have handled it, and the Lord knew that, so He gave me what I could handle (alongside Him) each and every day.

Lessons Learned

During this period, I traveled for work and had dinner with the CFO of a ministry I was serving. This amazing lady was in her late fifties or early sixties. She asked about what was going on in my life. I'll never forget our conversation. After I explained our situation, she looked at me and said, "You are learning lessons that I didn't learn until I was in my fifties." I made it clear that I would rather wait, but I did see how the Lord has used this and other "Glad I Didn't Know" stories to grow my faith and show me God's provision and love.

I've seen a video message Francis Chan did where he had a huge rope on the stage. He focuses the attention of the audience on how massive the rope is as it weaves across the stage a few times. He refers to that as eternity. Then he points at the very tip of the rope and refers to that as life on earth. It is a great reminder of time and was such an applicable lesson to me at a relatively young age. We lost Wayne when he was forty-two, but I believe he lived as much life as many ninety-year-olds. He recorded a video to be played at his funeral and basically delivered his own eulogy. He laid out the gospel and never whined or pouted about what life, or the Lord, had handed him.

I'm also thankful that in taking Wayne from us, He gave Bryan and me great friends in Ken and Jeanne. They had been wonderful friends to Wayne for years, and his illness brought us together. Ken had lost both his brothers, and Bryan lost Wayne. We are not a family by birth but definitely by choice.

The other lesson I learned was to change the way I discuss my plans. I used to commit to doing certain things. I was adamant and rigid. After this season, I changed my wording. Instead of saying "I will do that," I began to say, "I will plan to do that." It might have been so slight that some people didn't notice it, but for me, it was a complete shift in how I viewed things. It wasn't to be noncommittal but to remind me that I can control very few things, and I need to be prepared to pivot when circumstances change.

I'm glad I didn't know the pain that lay ahead, but I am also glad I realized it was for a season and that my challenge today is to live life in a way that reflects that reality. None of us is guaranteed any amount of time, yet we seem surprised whenever the end comes. May we do our best to share with others the importance of a relationship with Christ so they will be prepared for that day as well.

> "Who shall separate us from the love of Christ? Shall trouble or hardship or persecution or famine or nakedness or danger or sword? As it is written: 'For your sake we face death all day long; we are considered as sheep to be slaughtered.' No in all these things we are more than conquerors through him who loved us. For I am convinced that neither death nor life, neither angels nor demons, neither the present nor the future, nor any powers, neither height nor depth, nor anything else in all creation, will be able to separate us from the love of God that is in Christ Jesus our Lord" (Romans 8:35–39).

Questions to Consider

- What loss have you experienced in life that you can look back on and see how the Lord has worked in you since that time?

- If you were to do a video for your funeral, what would you say?

- What are the lessons you are learning now or have recently learned that you wish you could have waited until later in life to experience?

16

Another Loss

The spring after Wayne passed away, we were finding a new normal. We had an energetic and highly intelligent (every mom's description of her kids) two-year-old child. Then we found out I was pregnant, and we were excited.

I'm a CPA for a reason. I often tell people that if you did an MRI, you would find I don't even have the right side of my brain. I'm very left-brained, extremely analytical, and not a terribly emotional person. I'm blessed to have Bryan in my life for so many reasons, but one of those is to balance this one-sided approach. He has been known to say to me, "You know there will be people's emotions involved in this, right?" Whatever "this" happens to be in those circumstances, he's right.

It was for practical reasons that with each pregnancy we didn't tell anyone until after twelve weeks. I understand the likelihood of something going wrong to be much greater in the first trimester. If you tell everyone during that time and something happens, then you have to go back to each person and tell them that news as well. For me, it's just easier to wait.

We did wait, and at thirteen weeks, we told everyone our thrilling news. Our friends and family were nearly as excited as we were. That year, we had something to look forward to. It was an opportunity to move out of the season of grief and look forward with anticipation to a new life and a new sense of energy in our family.

After the previous year of juggling our jobs and traveling to care for Wayne, 2001 allowed us to focus on home, church, and work. I had been traveling for work, and the three of us were going to meet at our friend's house in Northern California. I arrived a couple of days before Bryan. The four of us had been through a lot the year before and were looking forward to just hanging out and enjoying each other's company.

I woke up the morning after I arrived to find I was bleeding. Surely this wasn't serious. I had only been pregnant once before, so I wasn't an expert. Hopefully, it was something minor, I thought, but I didn't know what to do so I called my doctor's office in Colorado. After asking several questions, they concluded it wasn't minor. They believed I was having a miscarriage, and there wasn't anything that could be done. I didn't need to go to the hospital right then. Nature would take its course.

So there I sat, in someone else's home, a thousand miles from mine, without my husband, going through what I would later determine was one of the most emotional times of my life. I was mourning yet another loss. The loss of a child, *our* child.

Our friends were amazing! You couldn't ask for more love and support. I, of course, told Bryan I was fine and would see him in a few days. They encouraged him to come sooner, which he did. Seeing him walk through their door unexpectedly is one of my life's best memories.

For anyone who's been through this ordeal, you know that's not the end of the story. There are follow-up appointments and procedures. I also had to take some shots that were a form of chemotherapy. Oh yeah, and we had to tell everyone I was no longer pregnant.

I mentioned at the start of this story how left-brained I am. What I discovered through this experience was a depth of emotion I had not experienced before—or frankly since. You know that thousands of people go through this every year, but they're not you. This is personal and real and deep.

Life slowly returned to routines, and the pain began to subside. Obviously, by including the story here, you can understand it was a time of life that shaped part of who I am, and I've learned we must move on. It seems others forget, but those of us who have experienced this never do.

Glad I Didn't Know

I'm glad I didn't know the journey that seemed so joyful and exciting would end with the loss of a child. I wouldn't have wanted to walk down that path from the beginning. We would have possibly taken measures after our first child was born to avoid having more children. After all, if you can avoid something painful, wouldn't you do it? That would have resulted in Bethany being an only child, and she and Kimberly are the best sisters in the world. How she would have missed out!

Lessons Learned

I have emotions. Who knew? They still don't show up often, but I realized in the days following this event that I was going through grief just like you would for the loss of any person who had spent time on Earth with you. The difference for me was that I felt like it shouldn't be that way. No one had met this child, so how could I have become attached?

This is a great reminder to me. It's not up to me to determine what should or shouldn't upset others. When people are going through a personally difficult time, I just need to be available to them. I don't have to (nor can I) fix it. It has given me the opportunity to listen and share with people in a way that can only be done when you share a significant experience.

I'm glad I didn't know this loss would follow our loss from just the year before. However, when I get to Heaven, I have a very special treat in store. I will finally meet our third child, whom I never had the opportunity to spend time with here.

> "He called a little child to him, and placed the child among them. And he said: 'Truly I tell you, unless you change and become like little children, you will never enter the kingdom of heaven. Therefore, whoever takes the lowly position of this child is the greatest in the kingdom of heaven. And whoever welcomes one such child in my name welcomes me'" (Matthew 18:2–5).

Questions to Consider

- What is the most emotional experience you've walked through in your life?

- Have you had a time when you were coming out of a difficult season only to have something you were looking forward to lost as well? How did God make Himself known?

- What does it mean to you to have "childlike faith?"

17

Seeking Asylum

Name Withheld

I was raised by two educated parents. My dad earned his master's degree at the University of Arizona in the '60s, way before I was born. My mom speaks five languages, including Italian, English, and Arabic. Even though my parents had many opportunities to migrate to the West, they chose to live in our African country, even during the terrible times of political instability that killed tens of thousands of innocent people. So, growing up, my parents instilled in me a sense of pride in who I was. That sense of national pride is the identity I passed on to my children.

When my son was four years old, we traveled to Norway to visit our dear friends, and when it was time to head back, he asked me why we couldn't stay there. He said our city was so dirty and the playgrounds were not so accessible, so he preferred to stay there, where it was so nice. I told him our city was our home; it was where God chose us to be. If we didn't like how dirty it was, then it was our job to clean it up. We wouldn't just abandon it.

Never in my wildest imagination did I consider this place I called home would make me choose between staying and going to prison or fleeing the country for an indefinite period.

It started with the advent of a new leader, who carefully cultivated the political elites' resentment toward the ruling party that had overseen our country's politics for thirty years. The resentment toward the ruling party and, by extension, the people of our region, stemmed from a retaliation that had been desired for twenty-five years. Finally, a civil war broke out, where the country's government, the state's government, and the militia from a neighboring tribe targeted our small region in the northern part of the country with only six million people. The people of our region were vilified and called names on public television. The vast majority of the population believed the narrative, and hatred toward our people mounted. Many, including church leaders, spoke about wiping out our identity and making the region insignificant. There was a communication blackout in targeted areas at the beginning of the war. Only months later did we hear about the horrific violence and the massacre that took place where my aunt lives.

Although we lived in the capital city, both sets of our parents were from the affected region. In addition, we ran two successful businesses in the capital, which made us visible to the people around us. A couple of months after the war started, government officials in civilian clothing came to our home inquiring about our whereabouts. They came when we were not home. We noticed our phones were tapped, and we started to receive calls from someone threatening us. Finally, we realized we had to leave when we heard that we, among many successful businesspeople from our region, were at risk of being wrongfully imprisoned for political reasons.

I remember when it became real that we had to leave our aging parents, our siblings, our church family, our thriving businesses, the wonderful mission school my kids were attending, and our comfortable home indefinitely. The realization didn't happen immediately, as our minds were focused on escaping the physical danger, but after we landed safely in the US and a few months passed, reality hit home. It happened so quickly that we did not have a grieving period. We needed to leave our country discreetly, so we left without saying goodbye. In all of this, God's provision was evident.

First, we left during the COVID-19 pandemic and needed a negative Covid report to make it to the plane. God did that. Many were stopped by immigration officers at the airport and prevented from traveling. Although the officer stopped us right when we were boarding the plane, somehow, he let us board it. God did that too.

In the US, God provided us with a friend who helped us find a house in an area with a reasonably good public school system. God also helped my husband get two significant certifications in one year: a project manager professional (PMP) and a professional engineer (PE). He then found a job that he still loves and in which he excels.

No one could have prepared us for the psychological struggle we were going to face as we dealt with the immigration system in the US. When our visitor's visa was about to expire, people advised us to apply for asylum, and not knowing how difficult that process was, we sent in our application.

We had anticipated getting an interview within the next three months so the immigration officer could hear our case and grant us an asylee status. This status allows us to apply for a green card, which is permission to work in the US permanently. It also allows us to travel outside of the US and be allowed reentry. In the event we missed family, we had hoped to meet them in Kenya or some other country. However, two and half years later, as I write this story, we have yet to have our interview. We are allowed a renewable temporary work permit every two years, but we are not allowed to leave the country. The renewal process is not straightforward, either. We continue studying the immigration system, how it works, and whether there is a different route to getting a green card, but every door we knock on seems to shut because we don't have the status to pursue these other avenues. Our only option is to wait in this state of limbo for years. We have heard of people who have waited seven years to get an asylum interview. That uncertainty is excruciating. Things most people do without thinking about are not available to us. I serve on the board of an international organization and cannot be physically present for some of their meetings and gatherings because of travel restrictions. Our job opportunities are restricted because of the limited number of employers willing to work with the immigration issues we present. Some people can't imagine if their parents or children didn't live in the same city, or at least the same state, while ours live over 8,000 miles away, and we have no ability to be physically present with them for the foreseeable future.

Yet, through all of this, we see God working.

Glad I Didn't Know

As you can imagine, it has been a nightmare of a situation. Not only did we unjustly lose our original home, but we now find ourselves in a foreign place that continues to remind us that we have no home. It is in this state of anxiety and depression that we turn to God in lament. We cry out to God like the Israelites did in Egypt and the wilderness. We often ask, "Why?" and "Where are you, God, in this?" The beauty of lament is that it moves us toward God rather than away from God and into despair. God often responds to these cries, not by taking the problem completely away but through small blessings that show us He still cares about justice and righteousness on this earth. It is just like the author of Psalm 42; when he laments, he is reminded, "By day the Lord directs his love—at night his song is with me—a prayer to the God of my life" (Psalm 42:8). The song at night for me has been this: Why so downcast, oh my soul, put your hope in God and bless the Lord, oh my soul!

Lessons Learned

I have a renewed sense of understanding about my identity. As I mentioned above, I placed a massive value on my national identity and associated my home with that identity. Although I didn't have high regard for my ethnic identity, the current environment in my home country required me to care about regional identity. These identities, national and ethnic, are God-given, and I have to wrestle with what it means to be these in light of my Christian identity.

Steve Bryan's book, *Cultural Identity and the Purposes of God*, has been an excellent resource for me. My conviction so far is that my ethnic and national identity is offered up to God in worship for the service of all peoples.

One thing that has drastically changed is my definition of *home*. Home is where God and God's people are. As I walk into our church building in the US, whether for choir practice or Sunday worship, I am engulfed with that sense of home. We have found it very difficult to find deep relationships that extend outside of the church. Still, I find deep connections even in the communal utterances of dedication and zeal for Christ.

Finally, in this season of waiting, I have learned that God does not tell us how long we are to wait before our prayers are answered or what challenges are before us, but He assures us that He will be with us every step of the way. Therefore, I am learning what it means to live one day at a time, and not to deprive myself of life's joy today by obsessing about tomorrow. I am learning to trust God for tomorrow because He is in charge and because He cares.[10]

---

10 The author of this story is a leader in business and nonprofit organizations globally. She serves in both management and board positions. We have withheld her name in light of the facts of this story. Please keep her, her family, and the difficulties she presents here in your prayers.

"I remain confident of this: I will see the goodness of the Lord in the land of the living. Wait for the Lord; be strong and take heart and wait for the Lord" (Psalm 27:13–14).

Questions to Consider

- Where do you find your identity, and is that ever problematic or challenging?

- What relationships do you have that provide a sense of community?

- If you have had to leave something behind suddenly, how did you deal with the grief and any bitterness?

18

2 Pounds, 8 Ounces

After significant challenges in 2000 and 2001, life was beginning to find a new rhythm. Work was going well for both of us, and Bethany was a joy. In late spring, we found out I was pregnant again, and we were cautiously excited about the next step for our family.

After Bethany found out we were going to have a baby, I remember she told us many times that she was praying for a sister. I can overreact out of concern and asked Bryan if we should be worried about how her faith would be impacted if God chose to give us a son. Fortunately, Bryan can see through my idiosyncrasies and reminded me she was three. He was pretty sure she would be fine.

We went through the summer months and enjoyed those days with Bethany as an only child, knowing life would change when January 16 (or so) rolled around. I joked that I must not be a very good CPA to have a child due sixteen days after the end of the year and miss out on claiming another exemption on our tax return because, in those days, children still provided a tax savings.

September 30 was Bryan's birthday. We went out for dinner and had a nice time. The next day was a Tuesday, and I worked at a client's office. Near the end of the day, I started bleeding. It was different from the year before but was still definitely not normal. As I drove home, I called the doctor's office to see what they thought. They suggested I go to the hospital to get checked out.

I went home, changed clothes, and told Bryan what was going on and what the doctor's office said. He suggested driving me to the hospital, but I told him that wasn't necessary. It was dinnertime and certainly what was going to happen was that we would sit in a boring room for hours with a three-year-old, only to find out we needed to go home. He understood my point, reluctantly agreed, and off I went.

The doctor did some tests and decided it would be best to keep me overnight. Bryan brought Bethany to the hospital so I could tell her goodnight, and we expected I would be home the next day. The following morning, the medical team decided I was having contractions, and having a baby four months early was not a good option. They gave me a magnesium medication that relaxes muscles. It was strange because it was so effective at relaxing all of my muscles that my eyes wouldn't focus.

The second day, several people from the office came by to visit and brought some things to keep me entertained. They stood or sat scattered around my room, and just as I would start to focus on one person, someone else would speak. I finally had to close my eyes and just listen. If you've ever experienced this medication, you know exactly what I am talking about. It was strange!

I spent three days at the local community hospital and then it was determined I should be transported by ambulance to a regional medical center. Otherwise, if I delivered our baby early, the baby would go to that hospital with a Level 3 Neonatal Intensive Care Unit (NICU), and I would have to stay at the current hospital. When the staff put it that way, the transfer seemed like a good idea. It was further away from our house and meant fewer visits or less time for each visit with Bryan and Bethany, but it was the best option available.

I am a planner (as previously disclosed) and after several more days in the hospital, I asked the doctor how long I would be there. I just needed to know. "If it is until January, that is fine. Just tell me." The doctor said I could go home. Bryan and I were surprised to hear this. No one had indicated that was even a possibility. The doctor added, "But if something happens, you'll die before you get to the hospital." Decision made. I would stay at the hospital until this baby was born. (Side note: In all of our dealings with doctors, we have found the more specialized they are, the less they "beat around the bush." They know their field well and don't feel it is necessary to sugarcoat anything. I appreciate this but recognize it can be offensive to some. I like the facts and the truth as it makes decision-making easier, even if it can be scary.)

I settled into the routine of only being allowed out of bed to use the restroom or one wheelchair ride per day. You know you've been cooped up for a while when you think, *I would love to go to the grocery store.* Or, *It would be great to wander around Walmart.* We planned Bethany's fourth birthday party with the help of some close friends, and my mom and stepdad came to town to celebrate on October 20.

Everyone's hope was for the baby to arrive as close to January as possible. On October 26, the doctor decided there would be no more waiting. They let the contractions start and scheduled a Cesarean section for the next morning at 7 a.m. I was transferred to a labor and delivery room for the night, on the most uncomfortable bed/cot ever constructed. I told Bryan the next day would be a long day so recommended he go home and get some good sleep. There was nothing the nurses needed to do. I stayed in the room by myself all night, without even a TV. I watched the red digital clock on the wall as each minute passed. Then something awful happened. The clock went 1:57, 1:58, 1:59, 1:00. What?! There must be something wrong. I had just gone through those sixty minutes.

Then I realized, *It's Daylight Savings time!* Here we go again: 1:01, 1:02, 1:03 . . . Ugh!

Morning came and the surgery went fast. The only additional complication, beyond having a baby twelve weeks early, was my heart rate dropped during the surgery. I had just enough medical training to know it wasn't good when certain alarms sounded. I asked Bryan what was going on, and all he said was, "Doctor?"

The anesthesiologist replied, "We're working on it." I found out later that my blood pressure had dropped to 50/30. I normally run low but not that low.

Kimberly came into the world weighing a whopping two pounds, eight ounces. Her arm from fingertip to shoulder was the size of Bryan's finger. She had no cartilage, so her ears were floppy and had to be smoothed back against her head when they moved her into any position. Her skin was translucent, so you could see her veins. She was so sensitive that we couldn't even touch her for a few weeks because it made her heart rate skyrocket.

We spent the next three months in the NICU, where the medical staff said they care for early babies and sick babies and our daughter decided to be both. She took advantage of every service the hospital offered. She had two surgeries, was on the ventilator twice as long as they wanted for any baby, set off countless alarms, and on and on. She couldn't maintain her temperature, so as she got older (six weeks or so), we had to wrap her in a towel and place her in a little tub where we would unwrap one limb at a time to bathe her.

One particular day, the staff was struggling because there were no more veins that would take an IV. They needed to get her medicine and nutrition into her. The only option was to cut down to an artery. They tried that with both arteries in her neck and one in her arm. They could do one more try with the other arm. If that didn't work, the outlook was bleak for her survival. A neonatal surgeon came in and successfully completed the procedure.

Those were long, hard days and nights. I'd wake up at 3 a.m. and call the hospital to check on Kimberly. Some nights, I would go right back to sleep; some nights, Bryan and I would discuss if she was going to live or not.

It didn't get better fast when she came home from the hospital. She couldn't leave the house, except for doctor's appointments, for four months. She was on a heart monitor until she was nearly ten months old and oxygen until just before she turned one.

One night, we had friends over for dinner. We heard Bethany casually say, "Kimberly, blue is not a good color on you." Our daughter had stopped breathing and had turned blue. Our friends were terrified, but it was a common occurrence for us, and we calmly helped her start breathing again. Who knew it was so hard to remember to take your next breath?

Eventually, she turned a corner and never looked back.

Five years later gave us a glimpse of how the Lord worked. We were moving to Southern California. We had selected the school the girls would attend, and on a house-hunting trip, we visited the school so the kindergarten teacher could do a readiness assessment with Kimberly. The rest of us were on the playground. The teacher brought Kimberly outside when she was finished and mentioned Kimberly had told her we were moving from Colorado Springs. The teacher said her best friend and the godmother of her daughter was a surgeon at Memorial Hospital. I asked her friend's name. When she spoke the name, I began to cry. It was the physician who had saved Kimberly's life with the arterial surgery. The Lord knew that five years later, we would move halfway across the country and His little girl would be placed in the kindergarten class of the surgeon's best friend. What an amazing blessing!

Kimberly should have a laundry list of significant problems, including vision problems, lung issues, heart problems, possible brain damage, and on and on. The only two—very minor—issues we can faintly attribute to her difficult and premature start to life are some loose ligaments and possibly some nerve endings that didn't fully develop, so she hates to be hugged. While that's hard for a mom who loves to cuddle, it is definitely not an issue to complain about and just results in a bit of teasing now as an adult.

Glad I Didn't Know

I'm glad I didn't know the incredible months of anxiety and emotional hardship that were ahead when I discovered I was pregnant again. Having come through a miscarriage, I am not sure that I would have been first in line to say, "Pick me. Let me spend thirty days in the hospital. Let me actively consider every day if my child will live through the next twenty-four hours."

That experience, like others you and I go through, has impacted some things for the rest of my life. I am glad they are over, but it is another reminder of the seasons of life. We went through *winter*, but we could rest knowing spring was on the way.

Lessons Learned

There are many lessons I learned during this time. The first was that there are times when you are too close to the situation, and you can rest knowing that other people are praying. We had people around the world praying for Kimberly. That was such a blessing when I wasn't sure how the next five minutes would go. I didn't approach the throne of grace with my list of requests. I just sat quietly in the arms of the Lord and allowed Him to wrap those arms around me and remind me He alone is God, and I am not.

I was also encouraged that God provided me with the strength I needed for my particular circumstances. I couldn't worry about tomorrow or sometimes even the next few hours. I just had to focus on what was happening now and how the Lord was there. Whether the result was what I desired or not did not make His presence more or less true. God will do the same for you today.

There are opportunities to minister all around us. The NICU was an incredible mission field to live out our faith day-to-day and let God use us as He saw fit. We were one of only a couple of intact families. There are many young moms by themselves or young grandparents now involved in raising another generation. For weeks, we had the ability to minister to the other families as well as the medical staff we saw daily. We found out the surgeon who performed both of her surgeries in the operating room was a believer who served as the medical director for an international medical ministry. He prayed for each of his patients before surgery. We were only made aware of that because someone gave me a book, which I read in the NICU. The surgeon saw it and commented that it was written by his former colleague. A discussion ensued about his work and his faith. Just another little encouragement to show that God cares about every detail.

Related to the fact that God calls us to have the faith of a child, remember Bethany's prayers? She and her sister have been incredibly close throughout their lives (please understand, they have certainly had their sibling moments). She may not have been eternally lost if the Lord had given her a brother, but she trusted Him to give her the sister she wanted so badly, and I didn't need to worry.

Finally, God orchestrates things in our lives that we may not know about for years to come, but He is in everything from the start.

"I praise you because I am fearfully and wonderfully made; your works are wonderful. I know that full well" (Psalm 139:14).

Questions to Consider

- Have you ever had a long-term opportunity to invest in people you didn't know and wouldn't see again?

- Can you think of a situation you encountered, where years later, you found out something that related to that situation, and you were amazed?

- When was a time the Lord provided someone with just the right expertise you needed for that particular situation?

19

Mark's Death

Chip Watkins

Our twenty-seven-year-old son, Mark, died unexpectedly on December 2. We knew he had been using off-market painkillers because of a compound leg fracture that had not been set properly, but we did not know he had been using other drugs. One night, he bought heroin cut with fentanyl. The next afternoon, his roommate found his lifeless body.

At 6:30 p.m. that evening, our daughter called me to say that two policemen had come to our home to tell us they had received word from the police in the community where Mark lived, that he had died.

Suffice it to say that my wife and our two surviving children were devastated. We had been drafted into a club that no one clamors to join. With no preparation, grief—the realization our expectations about the future would not be fulfilled—was instantaneous and intense. Our pastor dropped whatever else he was doing and came to sit with us for several hours that night.

Glad I Didn't Know

God calls us to look forward to the future. In Genesis 3:15 (ESV), God foreshadows our redemption: "I will put enmity between you [the serpent] and the woman, and between your offspring and her offspring; he shall bruise your head, and you shall bruise his heel." In the gospels, we read of the initiation of the Kingdom of God on earth, and Jesus's promise for our future, "And if I go and prepare a place for you, I will come again and take you to myself, that where I am you may be also" (John 14:3). Then, in Revelation 20–22, we receive the vision of the new heavens and the new earth—the future and complete fulfillment of the promises in Genesis 3 and John 14. However, Matthew 24:36 makes it clear that God does not reveal to us the day or the hour.

We anticipate many events in our lives, some common—daily time with our spouse and family, weekly corporate worship, our next day at work—and some not so common, such as graduations, weddings, the birth or adoption of children, celebrating holidays with family, and even the "timely" death of elderly relatives and friends. But can you imagine God revealing to you, say, five or ten years before the fact, and with complete certainty, that your child *will* die of a drug overdose on December 2 and the year, and there is nothing you can do to prevent his death? How you might dread the passing of each day, knowing you are one day closer to the death of your beloved!? How your anger at God might build over the days, months, or even years over how, in His providence, He would allow your child to die an untimely death. How Satan—that serpent of old—would use that knowledge to distract you from fulfilling the work to which God has called you in the meantime.[11]

---

11 Of course, some have that kind of knowledge, though not supernaturally revealed and usually without a certain date—most commonly, with the diagnosis of a "terminal" illness that will result in death within a relatively short time.

With that in mind, I believe God is gracious and merciful in withholding this kind of exact knowledge from us. He gives us grace to walk with Him each day, day after day.

Lessons Learned

Community is important: Our first actions after learning of Mark's death were to contact other people—our pastor, family, and close friends. Our church community, family members, and other friends poured out their love for us, visiting with us, praying for us, hosting our extended family in their home for a meal after the memorial service, bringing meals to us for months, traveling with me to clean out Mark's apartment, and caring for us in countless other ways. (When my brother arrived for the memorial service, he volunteered to wash our home's windows!)

Our "community group"—a small group of folks in our church that meets bi-weekly for fellowship, prayer, and Bible study (in that order)—closed around us and held a special meeting to pray for us. On Sunday mornings, other church members went out of their way to commiserate with us and comfort us.

Eight years later, I continue to be surprised that some still remember the date and send us cards or remind us they continue to pray for us.

God is faithful and good: This is perhaps a lesson not learned but one certainly reinforced in the wake of Mark's death. We do not know (and until we are in heaven, will not know) all of God's eternal purposes in Mark's death, but we do know that all things He brings into our lives work together for our good. The "good" to which Paul refers is not our earthly ease, comfort, or wealth but our conformity to the image of Christ through our calling, our justification, and, as those who have been justified, our sanctification and glorification in Christ (Romans 8:28–30).

Do not be afraid to be silent: People who feel compelled to talk often speak foolishly or insensitively. I cannot count the number of people who greeted me in the receiving line after Mark's memorial service who said, in effect, "I don't know what to say." My response was usually, "That's OK. There are no words." In those circumstances, *presence* is more important than words. There will be time for words later.

Grieve well: I have learned so much about grief because of Mark's death. As noted above, grief is our response to the realization that our expectations for the future will not be fulfilled, and in grieving well, we come, each of us through a unique journey, to accept that those expectations will not be fulfilled. Though we may grieve after many events—the loss of a friendship or a job, a divorce, or the failure to achieve a cherished goal—we typically grieve most deeply in the face of and after the death of a loved one, usually a parent, sibling, or child.

Our experience of grief attendant to death depends on our personality, the closeness of our relationship to the decedent, and the circumstances of the death. Was it a close relative or friend, or someone we knew only casually? If they were a relative, did we enjoy their company, or was it a difficult relationship, perhaps carried on out of duty but not affection? Did we spend much time with them? Did they die unexpectedly or after a long illness? Are we male or female? How easily do we adjust our expectations to changed circumstances? All these factors, and no doubt others, affect our experience of the intensity of grief. I cannot expect others to grieve in the same manner or with the same intensity (or lack of intensity) as I do.

To illustrate, both of my parents died "at a ripe old age" after illnesses—Dad from cancer and Mom from the effects of Alzheimer's disease. My brothers and I and our families began grieving when Dad and then Mom were diagnosed. Though we grieved their deaths, because their deaths were not unexpected, we had worked through much of our grief before they died. By the time they died, we had shed any expectations for the future and were comforted by the fact they were now "home" in heaven—and we would see them again.

In contrast, because Mark died both unexpectedly and at a relatively young age, our grief was immediate and, for months, intense. Though the intensity of our grief has waned over time, grieving is never "done." Grief still occasionally spikes, especially around the anniversary of Mark's death, at events or places he enjoyed, or when we gather with his sister and brother or with extended family. Then our consciousness of his absence is more palpable.

One of the most important ways that we deal with our grief is by *remembering* Mark. Many people try to deal with grief by "stuffing" it—trying to avoid remembering the one who died, never talking about him or her, or even pretending that he or she never existed. This is wrong. The Bible frequently calls us to *remember*, and so we do. We have a leather jacket he wore and that I occasionally wear. His brother now owns the car that once belonged to Mark. Pictures of Mark and pictures that he took are displayed in our home. (A picture of Mark and his brother is the wallpaper on my phone.) We thank God for the years He gave us with him and the memories we have of his life. Perhaps, most importantly, we love to tell and re-tell stories and hear stories from others about him—stories of things he said or did, of times together, and of his accomplishments. Ironically, stories of the past relieve the grief for an unfulfilled future.[12]

> "The Lord is my rock, my fortress and my deliverer; my God is my Rock, in whom I take refuge, my shield and the horn of my salvation, my stronghold" (Psalm 18:2).

---

12   Chip Watkins is married to Margie and is the father of three children, one of whom died unexpectedly in 2015. He lives in Arlington, Virginia; is a ruling elder in McLean Presbyterian Church, in McLean, Virginia; and is a lawyer in Washington, DC, working primarily with tax-exempt organizations.

Questions to Consider

- Has a close relative died unexpectedly or at a young age? How did you process your grief?

- Are you in a community—church, workplace, club, neighborhood, or family—whose members would support you if a tragedy were to occur in your life?

- Do you trust that God is good even when an unexpected tragedy occurs?

20

Wildfire

We made a major life change in 2008 and agreed to move our family from Colorado to Southern California. It was an adventure, and we were excited—mostly. We knew eighteen months before moving, and I had commuted for that time. When we told our eight- and four-year-old daughters about a year in advance of the move (so they didn't hear it from others), there was a mixed reaction. Our eight-year-old ran to her room crying, convinced we were ruining her life. She even left a note on our pillow that we were not allowed to move her to California and signed it "The FBI." Our four-year-old also disappeared to her room. When we went to check on her, we found her starting to pack her books. She was ready!

We worked with the movers and when the door was closed on the moving truck on moving day, we got in our minivan. It was the four of us plus my mom and stepdad. We had decided we would vacation our way out there, and then they would see where we lived and where I worked. It was a trip filled with good times, creating lasting memories.

Our arrival in Southern California came at the start of the summer. I jumped into work, and the rest of the family jumped into experiencing everything the area had to offer, including Disneyland, the beach, and Los Angeles Angels games. All of those things were less than thirty minutes from our house.

As a left-brained, analytical person, one of my keys to success for the move was to have everything unpacked and boxes gone as soon as possible. We did that in record time, and Bryan was extremely efficient at breaking down every box and taking them to the recycling place. We were settled long before school started in September.

In early November, my dad and his wife came to visit. Now, as with most families, it was good to have them, but it added some complexities and maybe even a little tension to our daily routine. On Saturday morning, we got up and moved around, and when everyone was ready, all of us but Bryan headed off to Walmart. I'm not sure if that is something you do when you have company, but they loved to shop, and I didn't. If they wanted to shop, at least I could get the things I needed for around the house.

We were there until almost noon. When we walked out of the store, I noticed a large plume of smoke to the east and commented, "I don't like the way that looks." I wanted to get home to see if there was any information about a wildfire. On our way back to the house, my dad and his wife spotted a rummage sale. It was impossible for them to pass one up if they were by themselves, and it brought an adult form of pouting if you passed one by when they were with you. I agreed to stop but told them to keep it short.

While they were perusing someone else's junk, which they hoped to make their treasure (though I kept reminding them they flew from Iowa and had to return the same way with limited luggage), I kept my eye on the sky. By the time we left, the entire sky was getting dark from the smoke, and I didn't like the looks of that smoke at all.

When we arrived home, I found Bryan in the backyard surveying the vanishing blue above us as well. After a short discussion, we determined it would make sense for everyone to have an overnight bag packed. I began that process while he did a few preventive things around the outside of the house. Soon after, we were notified that authorities had just given our area a voluntary evacuation order.

I packed more things. Unfortunately, we had done a phenomenal job of unpacking and the fact that we had broken down all the boxes and taken them to the recycling center became a rather unfortunate situation. Not a single box remained in the house. I started to fill laundry hampers, garbage bags, and anything else with volume. I asked Bryan if there were any things in particular he wanted packed, and he said he didn't know because he had never thought about it. I said, "You haven't?"

"You have?"

We made arrangements to stay at a hotel about forty miles away so we would be completely out of the smoke and loaded everything we thought we might need and anything we considered irreplaceable into the vehicles. As we did this, the police came through and told us we were now under a mandatory evacuation and needed to leave. I realized the minivan was only half full and ran inside to grab armloads of clothes and the bills hanging on the front of the fridge. I figured those things would make life easier if we didn't ever come back. I vowed not to pay the property tax bill in my hand until we determined if we had a house still standing in a few days.

As we drove away, I looked in the rearview mirror and saw Kimberly softly crying. I asked her what was wrong and found out she was sad because she had only been able to pick a couple of stuffed animals to come along. When I told her everything would probably be just fine, but if something bad did happen, it was only a month until Christmas and imagine the new toys she would get if the others were gone. I think she started to pray that we might lose the house!

We spent two days away, and the firefighters did an amazing job of containing the fire. No homes were lost near us, and we returned to signs of destruction in the area and a smokey smell in the house but nothing consequential.

Glad I Didn't Know

Our neighbors assured us that ever since the housing development had been built, around 1982, this had never happened. It wasn't much comfort as we considered the possibility of being homeless in a matter of hours. If we had known this would happen, we may have selected another home and missed out on the incredible opportunities we had to make friends and share the love of Christ with some amazing people. Maybe we would have still bought there, but we would have saved boxes and watched the sky, always expecting something and not being fully engaged in being where we were. We didn't know, and we will always treasure the time we spent in that neighborhood.

Lessons Learned

Every year, many people awake in the middle of the night to a house fire and have to get out with only the clothes on their backs and each other. We had a few hours to plan and pack. When we were done and our minivan was only half full, it produced a moment of realization. We are blessed with a number of material blessings, but even those things we consider important, such as photo albums and family heirlooms, only took up a little space. What truly mattered were the people. We have memories, and we can buy more stuff. That visual reminder, as I looked at the items we had packed, is something I will never forget.

> "Do not store up for yourselves treasures on earth, where moths and vermin destroy, and where thieves break in and steal. But store up for yourselves, treasures in Heaven,

where moths and vermin do not destroy, and where thieves do not break in and steal. For where your treasure is, there your heart will be also" (Matthew 6:19–21).

Questions to Consider

- Have you lost something valuable before? If so, how did it impact your life?

- Mentally walking through your house, what are the things you would take if you needed to evacuate quickly?

- Now consider the things you identified in the previous question. What makes them important?

21

You're Fired!

When the decision was made that I would leave the CPA firm and my twenty-year career, I only had four months to wind things down. I committed to not looking for a job or entertaining any offers during that time. I needed to finish well, and that required my complete focus on the task at hand.

When January rolled around, I began to think and dream and just give myself some space. I had worked since I was thirteen, and to not have the everyday commitment was strange but nice. I focused some of my quiet time on the concept of "Be Still."

I'm a list person, so I compiled a couple of lists. The first was of people who could speak into my life. These were individuals I respected and had enough of a relationship with that they knew me and could provide wise counsel. The second was ideas of opportunities I might like to pursue. These weren't jobs that were open but more general ideas of things that held an attraction for me. The ideas ranged from running a foundation and giving away money to being on a church's staff.

This was a sweet time. Bethany was wrapping up her senior year of high school and Kimberly her final year of junior high. I had more opportunities to just be Mom than I had in the past and enjoyed soaking up time with Bryan, myself, and the sun.

As I sifted through opportunities and listened to counsel, it was exciting and scary. Bryan and I had realized in the fall that we were likely moving yet had no idea where. The president of an accreditation organization located in Virginia had reached out that fall and again in December. Both times, I had said I wasn't going to consider anything until after December 31. The man actually flew to meet with us in January, and then I told him I needed time to wind down, be still, pray, and consider all my alternatives. He graciously laid out an offer and honored my request to not respond until April.

As I prayed and sought counsel, the focus on my future narrowed. As I was nearing a decision, I had three people in one week suggest I should consider this accreditation organization. The thing was that none of them knew anyone else had suggested it, and they didn't even know I was considering it. They just provided those unsolicited suggestions. It became clear that was where I needed to go.

I accepted the offer in April and then put them off again, saying I wanted to start on August 1. That gave us time to finish the school year, pack, and move across the entire country, from California to Virginia. We arrived four days before we needed to take Bethany to college in Kentucky. It was important to me that she knew where home was so when she drove back at Thanksgiving, she didn't go door-to-door asking, "Is this my home?" or "Are you my mother?"

Kimberly settled into her new school and joined a 4-H club where she became very active. Work started, and I loved it. We had a hard time settling into the community and a harder time finding a church home, which was difficult because we had come from an amazing church where we were plugged in and serving.

As time went on, we grew more accustomed to our new environment. We built a barn and put up fencing, and after years of riding other people's horses, Kimberly got her own horse to train and show and have on our property. I expanded in my role at the organization and took on more projects. I loved the staff and the member churches and ministries.

Then the world stopped for me one afternoon. Each of the individuals on the executive leadership team made monthly plans and shared them with each other. One of the other executive vice presidents was leaving, so I asked to meet with the president to go through my monthly plan before sending it to the others. I wanted to make sure it reflected the shift in responsibilities everyone would have. The president put off the meeting a few days, and then on the appointed day, he said he wanted to meet later in the afternoon. When the time came, he brought a folder into the conference room, which I thought nothing about. He started the meeting by informing me that people would probably think he was crazy, but he'd decided that was my last day with the company. I found out the folder contained my severance paperwork.

I was devastated! The myriad thoughts that went through my mind in the following minutes, hours, and days are still a blur. I felt failure and shame, shock and anger, confusion and frustration. Honestly, my most prevalent thought was that my family had moved from a place we loved to a place where we were struggling to settle—and for what? This!?

It took time to heal and recover. Mostly, I wanted answers to explain the why, which never came. If you go through something painful like that, you want to learn and grow from it so you can avoid it in the future. I felt like that closure never came. However, the results were still more than I could imagine, and the outpouring of love and support from personal and professional friends around the country was amazing.

I loved the organization and the people there—and still do. By God's grace, I have continued to maintain a professional relationship with the organization through my consulting practice and a personal relationship with many of the individuals who work there. The Lord protected my heart from bitterness, which I can truly credit only to Him.

Glad I Didn't Know

I am *so* glad I didn't know that I would lose the job that moved us across the country. I guarantee you, I would not have taken the job. The result of the move was that our youngest daughter had her high school years in Virginia, where she grew in amazing ways and had opportunities that would never have been hers in California. She thrived in ways that launched her into college and prepared her for the time beyond that.

I had been encouraged to start a consulting practice before I accepted this job. This was exactly what I needed to do just that.

Lessons Learned

I have to trust the process. The Lord sees all the results in advance. As a sports fan, I kind of see it like I have a role to play. The Lord, as Coach, sees how the role I play fits into the plans He has drawn up. I can't see that; I'm just looking at what is in front of me rather than the big field or court.

> "But be sure to fear the Lord and serve Him faithfully with all your heart; consider what great things He has done for you" (1 Samuel 12:24).

Questions to Consider

- What big surprise left you feeling hurt and angry, and how did you cope?

- How does your work life impact your personal life?

- How does your spiritual life impact your work life?

22

God's Timing Is Perfect!

James (Jim) West

As I reflect on 2022, I realize it was the best year of my life and that God's timing is always perfect!

On November 18, 2021, I passed the baton as executive director of a ministry called The Barnabas Group (TBG), which I had started twenty-one years before, and retired. My wife Suzy was retiring as COO and CFO of Christian Leadership Alliance. We were all set to spend our retirement years helping ministries as God opened doors and having fun traveling and enjoying life. Two weeks later, I had a tickle in my throat and went to see my doctor.

I praise God that I am fortunate enough to have Steve Cullen as my doctor. He cares about his patients and has a sense of urgency. Steve gave me some antibiotics, and when they didn't work after two days, he had me in an Ear, Nose, and Throat (ENT) doctor's office within one hour.

The ENT doctor told Suzy and me that I had HPV throat cancer and to go home and prepare my will and estate. As you might imagine, with

Suzy and me both retiring at the same time, our world turned in a quick direction we had not planned on!

I wouldn't want to relive 2022 but treasure every moment of it. God had His hand all over it. How can having cancer and facing the horrendous treatment throat cancer patients go through be part of the best year of anyone's life? Let me share with you the answer.

I grew close to the Lord. I had prayed for many years, asking Him to be drawn closer to Him. Cancer and the journey through it have taught me so much. When a doctor tells you that you have cancer, if you don't have a deep relationship with the heavenly Father, you will wish you did and work toward it. I had a good relationship, but that year brought me closer. I speak with Him far more often and am more focused on what He wants.

I found myself waking up early almost every morning and spending time just talking to God. It was an amazing time. Jesus was with me every step of the way—every moment. He allows trials into our lives to shape our character. He doesn't promise to take hardship from us but rather to walk through it with us.

A Bible verse I had often heard came alive for me. I probably prayed this verse hundreds of times each week, often while lying in the radiation tube for an average of forty-five minutes a session for thirty-five sessions. Joshua 1:9 says, "Have I not commanded you? Be strong and courageous. Do not be afraid; do not be discouraged, for the Lord your God will be with you wherever you go." It is now tattooed on my right arm. Romans 5:2–5 was also very important. "Through whom we have gained access by faith into this grace in which we now stand. And we boast in the hope of the glory of God. Not only so, but we also glory in our sufferings, because we know that suffering produces perseverance; perseverance, character; and character, hope. And hope does not put us to shame, because God's love has been poured into our hearts through the Holy Spirit, who has been given to us."

I grew closer to Suzy, my wife, too. We had always been very close. Now, most people would say we are joined at the hip. She carried me through this disease, the healing, and the recovery. I would never have made it through this without her. Running errands, buying food, making sure I took all the various medicines when I was supposed to, driving to treatments, and getting me to eat when I really didn't want to do anything—Suzy was crucial for me.

I also grew closer to my brother, Don. I saw him step up and take care of his "older" brother. He and his wife, Maggie, blessed us in so many ways.

I grew closer to many friends who prayed for us, cared for us, called us, sent incredibly thoughtful gifts, and prayed for us. That's not a typo; I mention *prayed for us* twice because you will never know how much this means until you are staring death in the face, and you see hundreds of people taking you and your condition to the Lord.

God surprised us in many ways, showing us He had everything under control. I share two of the most powerful examples of this.

The first thing happened the day after I was diagnosed with HPV throat cancer. I contacted an old friend who had also fought throat cancer and who was on the board at MD Anderson (MDA) in Houston. He made a call, and forty-five minutes later, I received a call from MDA. They gave me my patient number and had me scheduled for three days of meetings and tests the following week. What a blessing to get into MDA that quickly! The three doctors I met with during my initial visit gave me confidence that we would beat this disease.

The second way we saw God's hand on this journey happened right after we decided to go back to Houston for treatment. It would take about two months and meant a huge disruption in our lives. We had a friend who house-sat and cared for our dogs during that time. We wondered about where we would live during those two months. Several friends connected us with people in Houston, trying to find us a home. We checked many furnished places for rent, and they were all about $5,000 per month. A friend sent an email to a few people he knew in Houston, and they forwarded it on to others.

This email landed in Bonnie Miller's inbox. She read it and thought, *I know a Jim West in California. This couldn't be the same person, though.* We had served together on the board of a ministry for about fifteen years. She reached out, and she and her husband, Bill, offered us a room they had built over their two-car garage for their son when he went to college. It had a bedroom/living room, a small kitchen, and a bathroom! We excitedly accepted their gracious offer of a free place to stay, but it was so much more. Bill and Bonnie are strong followers of Christ and ministered to us every day. Bonnie was a friend Suzy could open up to over a glass of wine in the evening. My best memory of many great ones of Bill is him carrying me to our car when I had fainted, too weak to walk from the blood clots in my lungs and leg. Bill and Bonnie were angels and the hands of the Lord.

When you finish treatment, you get to "ring the bell." I rang the bell on March 25, 2022. They warned me the next few weeks after treatment ended would be the roughest time of all. They were right! I was down to 156 pounds and very weak. I was on oxygen and in a wheelchair. I had AFib and blood clots in my legs and lungs. I was afraid to shower without Suzy there in case I fell. Then I walked through my front door on April 1, 2022, after two months in Houston.

Many side effects come from radiation and chemo. The doctors can't tell you which side effects you will suffer. They can't tell you how long they will last or if they will be permanent. Each person is different. I have a few, but God is still using me and blessing Suzy and me.

Glad I Didn't Know

I am glad I didn't know that God had this speed bump in front of me. It was hard to give up the leadership of a ministry I had started from scratch and then worked at for twenty-one years and had watched God grow and bless. I had prepared myself mentally and strategically for several years to pass the reins, but I still wasn't as ready as I had hoped. Cancer completely took my mind off TBG!

Lessons Learned

The first lesson is having a well-developed relationship with our Lord Jesus *before* you need it! Don't wait as horrible tragedies can come out of nowhere and hit us when we least expect it. Start getting as close as possible to Jesus now.

Where you will spend eternity becomes a "real question" when the doctor tells you that you have cancer. I was not afraid to die. I slept well—very peacefully. Don't wait to make this decision for yourself. When the battle comes, it will come quickly and surprise you. If you haven't made a firm decision by then, you have made your decision.

Many people have asked me if I asked the "why" question at this time. "God, why did you allow this to happen to me? I have led a good life." All of us have sinned and are subject to the trials, tribulations, and diseases this world brings our way. Each day we live without something challenging going on in our lives is a gift from the Lord. Grace is getting something we don't deserve, and mercy is not getting what we do deserve. I, like everyone else on this planet, have sinned. I have probably sinned more than most. All of us will die one way or the other. When and how are the questions, not why. Even more important than when and how, though, is *where* will we spend eternity. This is the most important question we will ever have to answer!

The second thing I learned is you can't go through what we did, facing this cancer and being treated for it, without someone who loves you and will care for you. Suzy is that for me. I wouldn't have made it through without her. We saw hundreds of people at MD Anderson being treated, and all of them had someone with them to help them on their journey.

You can't hear everything the doctor says, ask all the right questions, run the errands you need to, or hold yourself accountable during these trials.

The third lesson is that the prayers of the saints are powerful! A few thousand people followed us on Caring Bridge and prayed for us. Many were followers of Christ, and many were not. People had their Bible studies and friends praying for us. Their prayers were more precious than gold to us. They gave us a reason to fight, and I know God heard them. We felt them! When someone asks you to pray for them, please do. It is serious spiritual business.

When you claim to be a follower of Christ and go through something like this, people are watching you to see what you really believe and where your faith is placed. I saw people accept Christ because they watched me go through this battle and saw Who I trusted in and how I leaned into Jesus.

A fourth lesson comes to mind when people ask me what I could have done to better prepare myself for this battle. My response is, "Memorize Scripture ahead of time."

I constantly prayed verses while being treated, especially while being locked into the mask in the radiation machine. Because I had opted for a special clinical trial that combined an MRI (so they could better direct the radiation) with the radiation, my average time locked in the mask in the radiation tube was more than thirty minutes longer than the typical time of ten to fifteen minutes. My stays in the tube lasted between a "quick" thirty-four minutes to two sessions a bit over ninety minutes. What I had in my mind was all I could focus on during that time. How important it is to be able to think on things that are "true, and noble, and right, and pure, and lovely, and admirable," as it says in Philippians 4:8.[13]

---

13   James (Jim) West has several world championships in Jiu Jitsu and multiple national championships in Sambo and Judo. He was a mortgage banker who went on to co-found The Barnabas Group and lead The Pocket Testament League. He and his wife, Suzy, have traveled and hiked extensively around the world and have a heart for connecting people and sharing Christ.

"Truly my soul finds rest in God; my salvation comes from Him. Truly He is my rock and my salvation; He is my fortress, I will never be shaken" (Psalm 62:12).

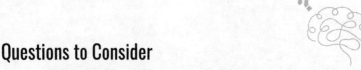

Questions to Consider

- What would your first action be if you were told to go home and get your will and estate ready?

- Is your relationship with Jesus established and ready to encounter a difficulty like this?

- When you say you will pray for someone, do you treat it like serious spiritual business?

23

Dream Job

When my time at the accreditation organization ended, I had no idea what would be next. We had moved our family away from where we loved to a place we were having a hard time settling. I have worked with churches and Christian ministries all my life. Aside from the organization I was no longer a part of, there were one or two small ministries in town. I had no desire to commute ninety minutes each way to Washington, DC, and the pandemic had not yet happened, so working remotely was not a typical mode of operation.

I treated this time as another sabbatical. My house was cleaned from top to bottom, including closets and storage areas. That was incredibly satisfying, but then it was done, and the pay wasn't very good—other than the pieces of spare change I found along the way. I thought there may be the possibility of returning to the accreditation organization if a coming change in leadership took place, so I waited. I enjoyed horse show season with our youngest daughter and went to visit our oldest daughter and watch some of her college volleyball games in the fall.

I knew that wouldn't last forever, so I often contemplated what the next chapter might hold. This change forced me to reevaluate something people had encouraged me to do for a few years. Several people had suggested I start a consulting practice. I told them I was too left-brained and analytical. I wanted to know that I had a steady paycheck on the fifteenth and thirtieth of every month. I was concerned about the possible volatility of work and income.

However, as we considered all of the options available, Bryan encouraged me to launch on my own, knowing it might be a year before it became a self-sustaining endeavor. With our girls nearly out of the house, the impact would be less if we needed to make some lifestyle changes based on income. It was also a time we could make changes in travel schedules as well. With kids not at home (or soon not to be), we could travel together when I had business that took me away from home.

We made the decision in November, and within a month, I had my first client. As I was meeting with the international director and the board chair, they asked how much of my time they could have upfront as there were many things to work through. I paused, kind of laughed, and said, "All of it." I didn't have another client, so my time was theirs.

That job launched my practice and provided all the income we needed. I devoted additional time, but as that time grew less, I found the ideal balance I desired of serving three ongoing clients and one portion of my time set aside for special projects. Today, this allows me to work with many different organizations in short segments. I tell people I spent the first twenty-two years of my career telling organizations what they needed to do better, and now I get to help them do it. It's so fun!

That leads me to share something I have discovered over the years while working with organizations. We sometimes keep people in positions where they are not gifted because we are trying to be nice. However, I don't think the Lord allows us to find joy in work where He has not equipped us. When someone is in a position where they are not thriving, it is impacting four people and organizations:

1. The individual who is not where they are supposed to be.
2. The organization they work for that doesn't have the right person.
3. The organization where they are supposed to work that doesn't have the right employee.
4. The person who is supposed to have that job can't because the position isn't available.

Glad I Didn't Know

While people had tried to tell me I should consult, I didn't trust my skills or the Lord's provision until He opened the door and shut all of my escape hatches. I'm glad I didn't know how easily the consulting practice would come together, though. I would have jumped into it and missed out on the true opportunities of trusting the Lord and seeing Him provide.

Lesson Learned

Others see you better than you can see yourself. I realize I need to not only continue to have outside input for my life, but I need to trust what they sense and what they see. In this case, it was a very fulfilling career move.

I have carefully considered why some leaders fail after a long and productive career and have decided one of the key factors is the lack of people speaking truth into their lives. I pray this lesson that I have learned will be applied as I move into the final stages of my career. May I be open to the truth that people around me are speaking (and may they speak it loudly and not be afraid to do so). It is through their insights and the Spirit's leading that I will continue to finish well.

"Where no counsel is, the people fall: but in the multitude of counselors there is safety" (Proverbs 11:14, KJV).

Questions to Consider

- Are you thriving in the work you do? How?

- If you're not thriving, what could you do to move in a direction that God might be calling you?

- Who are the counselors that speak truth to you?

From Military to Missions

Jerry White

In 1986, I was selected as the third international president of The Navigators, directly following thirty-year President Lorne Sanny, who had succeeded the founder, Dawson Trotman. My selection caught me totally by surprise since I was convinced the next president should have overseas missionary experience.

The story goes back thirteen years. Before joining The Navigators full-time, I had a fruitful career in the US Air Force. I had earned a PhD and was teaching Astronautics at the United States Air Force Academy while leading our Navigator ministry at the Air Force Academy as a layman.

When Lorne Sanny asked Mary and me to join the staff full-time, we considered it and, after much prayer, did so in 1973. I was thirty-five, with children, stepping out in faith, leaving my comfortable government salary for no guaranteed salary in a faith mission.

I began in the role of regional director. In that position, I unexpectedly encountered several interpersonal conflicts among staff, which

I worked tirelessly to solve. I traveled constantly and worked myself into a negative emotional hole. It soon caught up with me, resulting in burnout at age forty. It was known to everyone in the Navigator leadership. I believed my "press clippings"—that I was a person of great capacity and having an ability to solve problems. In reality, I was operating much in the flesh. I realized that later, rationalizing I was walking with God and serving Him. I was in so many ways. However, I was also depending on my natural skills and capacity. It took me several months to recover and get well. Then we moved west to take another region. I had learned some hard lessons. Most of them were insights into my life, as well as my leadership style.

Life was going well and the work and ministry in the region prospered. Then Lorne Sanny asked me to move back to our Colorado Springs headquarters to become his COO, or executive director. The idea was to lift some of his load and extend his presidency. It was a new position, so we had to figure out the boundaries between our roles, leading a staff of about 2,500 in over eighty countries. I was to handle day-to-day operations, while Lorne concentrated on strategic issues. Almost every leader then reported to me rather than Lorne, and most were older and far more experienced than me. Obviously, this was intimidating and, at times, a bit confusing as to who was really leading. It was a wonderful scenario for failure, but God gave great grace, and the international leaders did as well.

I had expected this to last about five years, but in my third year in that role, Lorne walked into my office and said, "Thirty years is enough. I am going to step down." That ignited a well-crafted selection process. I was tasked with implementing it. The process had to be completed within ninety days of Lorne's public announcement.

The members of the selection council of senior international Navigators and board members had been designated two years earlier. About a month before the selection council, I realized I could be a candidate. It really frightened me. I did not think I was qualified, knowing I had not been a missionary and realizing that my military background might not be the best fit for a large international organization. In many countries, the military is feared, not respected.

Long story short, I was selected on the first ballot. I had to surrender my desires and opinions. It was a sobering time. How could I possibly replace an icon like Lorne, who really put The Navigators on the evangelical map, growing from just over 100 staff to over 2,500 staff? Perhaps the best thing was knowing that I was not qualified and would need a strong team who was more gifted and experienced than me.

I knew there were tensions in the international work, having seen them firsthand in many council meetings and personal interactions. I had no comprehension of their extent, though. I remember my first international council meeting as president. The meeting was chaos. There was lots of pent-up criticism of being too "American," too controlling, too guided by the center at our headquarters. I finally stepped out of the chair role for the meeting and asked one of my vice presidents to lead while I just sat and took notes on the comments and complaints. I had to realize they were not criticizing me but were releasing feelings they could not express to a revered thirty-year-long leader. I was a good target. That began a multi-year process of decentralization of authority and decisions. We gave the emerging non-Americans much more of a say in our direction. It was not easy since it countered our tradition and history.

God gave me patience and a wonderful team. We made great progress. In the meantime, I was promoted to brigadier general in the Air Force Reserves (another surprise). I had actually planned to retire as a colonel, but Lorne counseled me, "Don't turn that down too quickly because you don't know what God might want to do." Clearly, that put me under more pressure.

In 1990, life was going well personally, in The Navigators, and in my Air Force Reserves career. Then life forever changed.

Mary and I were speaking at a Gaither conference in Ohio. Early on the morning of April 27, 1990, just as I was about to leave the hotel to speak, the phone rang. It was my executive assistant. She said, "Jerry, I am sorry to tell you that your son, Stephen, was murdered at his job late last night." That began a nightmare for our entire family. That story is fully told in Mary's book, *Harsh Grief, Gentle Hope*. Our lives were turned upside down. Police, publicity, an arrest, and a trial engulfed us. I was paralyzed. My team took over running The Navigators. Close Covenant friends took over our lives to help us through this time. Within hours, the three couples flew to Colorado Springs. They protected us, dealt with the media, and helped us navigate these terrible times. Many, many people prayed for us, lifting us to the Father.

Three weeks later, we had a scheduled Navigator international council meeting in Cyprus. I was in no shape to go. Lorne Sanny and veteran Navigator missionary and leader, Doug Sparks, and my team encouraged Mary and me to go. We needed it. Our staff needed it. So we went. A miracle of unity, prayer, and support surrounded us, though hurting as we were. Suddenly, I was not a PhD, general, and president. I was a broken, hurting parent and follower of Jesus. A friend, not just their leader.

We got through this time, by God's grace. It *appears* in hindsight that God used Stephen's death to unite our diverse Navigator staff and opened the door for a renewed season of leadership. God led me in that role for the next fifteen years. Our lives were transformed. My leadership was put through the fire of suffering. God did a work in and through us (and I say "us" because Mary was integral to my leadership and relationships among the staff) that was far beyond and deeper than anything I could have imagined. Our 3,000 staff worldwide, our board, and my leadership team responded to work together for our common mission.

Isaiah 41:10 says, "So do not fear, for I am with you; do not be dismayed, for I am your God. I will strengthen you and help you; I will uphold you with my righteous right hand." The international tensions did not disappear, but our godly leaders grew and led. It was not because of me or my team. It was God and the Holy Spirit working through our weakness. These weaknesses were so apparent. We faced them with trust and confidence that God would unify us.

In 2001, we called for a gathering of international leaders to meet in Cyprus again, to take a clean sheet of paper and ask God to give us direction for the future. We needed to determine who we were and what God was calling us to do as Navigators. I sat back and allowed them to work without interference from me. We saw the Holy Spirit speak to, guide, and unify us, ultimately leading to what is now our calling,

> *To advance the Gospel of Jesus and His Kingdom*
> *Into the Nations, through spiritual generations*
> *of Laborers, living and discipling among the Lost.*

This calling, along with nine core values and an essay depicting what all this looks like in practice, concluded for me a fifteen-year search to see our worldwide staff unified and working together. It was God's doing through seeking and suffering. It was not just me. It was hundreds of staff, many men and women who also suffered personally, humbly seeking God for direction.

Glad I Didn't Know

I am glad I did not fully know the tensions in the work that I would face. I am also glad I did not know the incredible pressure that faced me and our team at a personal level. Would I have followed through on what God called me to do had I known what was ahead? I don't know. Part of not knowing opened an avenue of trust and faith that no strategic plan could achieve.

I am glad I did not know that my son would die. While the grief that followed was overwhelming, I can't imagine knowing something so traumatic was coming. "Even though I walk through the darkest valley, I will fear no evil, for you are with me; your rod and your staff, they comfort me" (Psalm 23:4). We're thankful for the time we had with Stephen and the ways the Lord has worked since that horrible day. It is now a constant reminder that we "do not know what a day may bring forth." Suffering shaped my character and dependence on God. I was no longer the big leader but an ordinary believer who had to trust God in the most difficult of personal times.

I am glad I did not know the refining Mary and our family would go through. There are many ways for us to go deep with God. The pressure of suffering, when responded to in a godly way, molds us into usable and beautiful vessels for God's glory—precious things that go through extreme pressure or heat to get them to the point they are usable and beautiful. The mystery of not knowing is always present, but when difficult issues hit us, we are either paranoid or trusting. Fear gives way to confidence in God's sovereign and loving care. It is true of us as well. Yet we typically want to avoid the refining if possible.

Lessons Learned

I may find myself ill-equipped for certain tasks, yet that vulnerability is exactly what the Lord uses to keep me in a posture of dependence. It allows me to give Him the glory. As Isaiah 46:10 says, "I make known the end from the beginning, from ancient times, what is still to come. I say 'my purpose will stand, and I will do all that I please.'" It also gives me the peace of mind to know the results are not my responsibility. I am only responsible for my obedience.

Through each of these moments, I have been reminded of the importance of people. I've been blessed to have people who have challenged me professionally. I've had people who have supported me personally. I've also had people who helped me develop spiritually. That has given me a passion for doing this for others. I want to take the lessons I've learned and the people I've met and try to connect them and help others fulfill their calling.[14]

> "Come to me, all you who are weary and burdened, and I will give you rest. Take my yoke upon you and learn from me, for I am gentle and humble in heart, and you will find rest for your souls. For my yoke is easy and my burden is light" (Matthew 11:28–30).

Questions to Consider

- There are several aspects to this story. What struck you the most?

- If you were asked to give up your known and stable lifestyle for the uncertainty of missions, how would you respond?

- How are you using your experiences to invest in others?

---

14   Jerry White is a highly respected leader whose experiences and insights are sought after at the highest levels of the military and in ministry. His biographical information is longer than this chapter. He is a former associate professor of Astronautics at the United States Air Force Academy and a recognized expert in astrodynamics. He retired as a major general from the United States Air Force. Whether as a general, an organizational president, a national handball champion, or a friend, anyone who has the opportunity to have a conversation with him is fortunate.

25

How Much Can Happen in One Year?

We all have "those" years. I have written about a couple of others earlier. The year 2021 was one of those for us. It wasn't all bad, but it was full of significant changes and some challenges.

The year began with my dad's Parkinson's-related hallucinations escalating to an intolerable point. He had suffered with them for years, but they were initially infrequent and what you might refer to as "friendly." He would see someone who had maybe been dead for over a hundred years and have a conversation with them. Then the hallucinations progressed in frequency, and by early 2021, many were terrifying. For example, one day, he was convinced there were people in his room who were going to detonate a shrapnel bomb. This was during the COVID-19 pandemic, and we had a very difficult time getting an appointment with a doctor. When we finally did, they put him on medication, which he responded to very quickly, and life settled down.

Things were quiet for a couple of months leading up to our oldest daughter's college graduation. We were preparing to drive from Virginia to Kentucky on the morning of April 30 when my mom called. She's an early riser, but it was about 5:30 a.m. her time, which is early even for her. In a weak voice, she told me she had woken up a friend to get her and take her to the emergency room. After further inquiry, I found out that two days before, a horse had reared and fallen on top of her. You know a lot by the tone of voice your loved ones use. I knew she was not in good shape. So now what? We were about to embark on a seven-hour drive, during which, for about four hours, there would be no cell signal. Realizing there was nothing I could do, I prayed, and we left.

That day was touch-and-go as she ended up in emergency surgery that lasted several hours. We found out that if she had waited only two hours longer to go to the hospital, she would probably not have survived (nurses, don't be strong and stubborn; go to the hospital!). I chose to stay in Kentucky and attend Bethany's graduation ceremony and reception. You only get one shot at that. In addition, it turned out that Bethany's boyfriend asked if he could have our permission to propose to her when the time was right. What a Saturday!

On Sunday morning, I left Kentucky and went straight to South Dakota. I ended up there for the month of May, but Mom's recovery was nothing short of miraculous. I went back in September for her follow-up surgery, but she went from the ICU to riding horses again in only several months.

In June, our youngest daughter graduated from high school. We were supposed to take her graduation trip to Canada, which was her dream. Again, COVID-19 impacted that, and we weren't able to enter that country. We scrambled and had a great final vacation as a family of four (we look forward to family vacations as a bigger family in the years ahead) to Lake Placid.

July found us selling our house and downsizing to a townhouse to give us more flexibility as empty nesters. Our home purchases had always been to bigger places, so this exercise in sorting and culling was difficult. There were a few times when I said in exasperation, "I'm supposed to be twenty years older before I have to do this!" It was the right decision, but it was not easy.

November came and Andrés had indeed proposed to Bethany; they got married in a beautiful ceremony. It was a special time, but in a matter of six months, we had gone from one of our two precious girls being ours to being independent and married. Seasons of life are great, but sometimes the sentimental side of you struggles a little.

Throughout the fall, my dad continued to decline physically and mentally. He found himself in the ER several times, including both on Thanksgiving and Christmas. The year 2021 spilled over into 2022, and in January, he went into the hospital for the last time. Ironically, my maternal grandmother was also failing physically, though Alzheimer's had taken her mentally from us a few years before. She and my dad passed away within two hours of each other and in two different parts of the US.

Glad I Didn't Know

I tell you all of this because we've all been there. We have probably all sat at a stoplight and looked around and thought, *That person is having such a "normal" day. Why is my life in such turmoil or chaos right now? No one understands what I'm going through.* We didn't go into the year thinking all of these things would occur. We only knew about the two graduations.

Can you imagine the planning frenzy I would have gone into if I had known all of these things would happen? As I mentioned before, I would have tried to dissuade my mom from having that horse, which very likely would have caused a strain on our relationship. I might have asked for the kids to get married later—like my schedule was all that mattered. We might not have bought the home that has been exactly the right place to be for the next season. The Lord knew all that lay ahead, and He chose to reveal to me only what I could handle and trust Him for a little at a time.

Lessons Learned

There were great things, and there were really hard things that year. I would say the biggest lesson was that sometimes I can only decide for right now, and I can only do it with the information I have before me. I like to weigh all of my options, consider all the implications, and brain-storm what-if scenarios. I like to see how it will impact those around me. I always like to keep my options open, so I get concerned about making a decision that will limit my options later. Sometimes, you just have to trust the Lord for where you are and let Him worry about where you're going. Do the best you can with what you have and give yourself the freedom to decide what you need to decide now.

Interestingly, I learned a story about bitterness as well. I mentioned briefly that my dad and my maternal grandmother died within two hours of each other. She never forgave my dad after he and my mom were divorced. She harbored a lot of bitterness toward him.

While my grandma was not communicative, my aunt was always good about talking to her and giving her updates. She mentioned that my dad was in the hospital and in very serious condition. During that week, we were told at one point that my grandma would likely not make it through the night. She did and the next and the next. She labored for each breath and fought. I let my aunt know when my dad passed away. She called the facility where my grandma was and told them she was on her way over but to please tell my grandma, "She won." Before my aunt could get there, the staff told her, and she passed away. She held that bitterness until her last breath! It was a drain on her and caused her such pain. May I carefully consider my relationships and my attitudes to be certain they don't cause me or others unnecessary pain.

I was also reminded that you need to celebrate the blessings and highlights and not let the troubles of life get in the way. I don't always make the right decisions, but going to the college graduation instead of to the hospital was the right decision that day. I don't want to miss out on the good times the Lord provides while I focus on the difficulties of life around me. Sometimes He gives us memories for a lifetime, and sometimes, it might just be the momentary reprieve we need to face the next decision or challenge. Don't miss it.

> "When you pass through the waters, I will be with you; and when you pass through the rivers, they will not sweep over you. When you walk through the fire, you will not be burned; the flames will not set you ablaze" (Isaiah 43:2).

Questions to Consider

- What year(s) can you look back on as monumental in your life?

- What was the event or season when it seemed life was normal for everyone but you?

- Do you have a decision to make now in which you just have to use the information you have and trust the Lord with the rest?

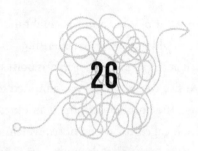

26

Logan's Story

Cari Arnold

The fact that God is faithful to keep his promises has become a grounding and unwavering pillar in my life. The journey to this place began when my firstborn son, Logan, was diagnosed with a chronic medical condition as a newborn.

After an adventurous birth, where his heart temporarily stopped, and we were rushed into the operating room, I thought the most traumatic part of becoming a new mom was behind me. Five weeks later, when Logan spiked a fever, we were sent to the emergency room and quickly learned he was critically septic, and if we had brought him a few hours later, it would have been too late. What would unfold in the weeks, months, and years ahead was scary and unbelievably hard. If I had the choice, I would not repeat any of it. I would not have endured the pain, fear, and tear-filled nights. I would also not have a deep trust in my Lord or an abiding love for His nearness through hardships. While I would absolutely have chosen to skip the pain if I could, I am also thankful that the Lord brings beauty out of ashes and has taught me wonderful things about Himself that I would not otherwise cherish.

We didn't know it at the time, but Logan was born already experiencing kidney failure. At five weeks old, he was admitted to the hospital for treatment and testing. The hospital performed an ultrasound to rule out a rare kidney condition called hydronephrosis, which only about 1 percent of children are born with. The ultrasound revealed that Logan had it. We were shocked, but the doctor assured us that most kids diagnosed with it only have a mild case and grow out of it with time. A follow-up test revealed that his condition was not mild. He had grade 5 out of 5 in both kidneys—it was as bad as it could be. Again, we felt overwhelmed by this news, though we didn't yet know how drastically this was going to shift the trajectory of our lives.

As uncertain and stressful as this new information was, God felt very near to us during this time. While we were in the hospital, our church community came around us and cared for us, including making hospital visits, bringing us food, taking care of our dog, and providing for us in ways that we hadn't even asked for. There were people around the world praying for Logan, many whom we'd never even met. The power of knowing you are being lifted up in prayer by such a widespread community and taken care of physically is so deeply encouraging and humbling.

Because of the severity of Logan's condition, he was referred to a specialist at the local children's hospital. The doctor immediately recognized there was a critical part of Logan's diagnosis missing and ordered a repeat test that day. He called us twenty minutes later while we were in the car on the way home and told us to turn around and come back because he needed emergency surgery that day.

While hearing that your child has a chronic medical condition is scary, being told that your eight-week-old baby needs emergency surgery is even scarier. As we turned around and headed back to the hospital, we were told not to feed him since he would be going straight into surgery. This worried me since he usually ate every two hours, but we did as instructed. It took a long time to get him into the operating room, and he ended up going six hours without eating. I was so anxious and didn't know what I was going to do when he woke up crying because he was hungry and I was not allowed to feed him. To my astonishment, he stayed asleep the entire time. It was the longest he had ever slept by far, and he didn't do it again for another six months. It felt like the Lord's clear provision in that moment. It was a reminder that He was there with us and that He was taking care of us in the details. The fear and heartache that came with seeing my child in pain did not change, but I was reminded that the Lord was right there with us in the midst of it.

Logan was monitored closely. His condition continued to worsen and was more complex than we originally thought. At four months old, he needed a second, more invasive surgery. The procedure included cutting a hole in his side, which allowed the kidneys to drain directly out into his diaper, relieving pressure on the kidneys and the entire system. This meant adding extra padding to his diapers, which doubled the price of diapers and also made diaper changes more complex than normal—and not something just anyone knew how to do.

This seemed to be the pattern of how Logan's medical journey went for the next year and a half. At every turn, things continued to get worse, and at every appointment, we received bad news. After his second surgery, he went on multiple medications, followed up with specialists regularly, and had frequent blood draws, catheters, and tests.

As a first-time mom who—I would later learn—was also dealing with postpartum depression, I was a wreck through all of this. I was anxious about his health and hyperaware of any little thing that seemed wrong, as I was always on the lookout for possible infections. I came to expect bad news since that had become the pattern. Our new normal of parenting was giving medications, navigating frequent appointments, and avoiding certain things, like going to the beach, so he wouldn't get sand in his opening, which was a sacrifice since we lived in Southern California. The surgery helped Logan's condition immensely, stabilizing him and allowing his body to begin to heal. This was a huge relief and perhaps the first good news we had received since he was born.

So many times we thanked God for access to incredible medical care because of where we live. Logan's surgeon is a world-renowned pediatric urologist. Families travel from other countries to see him, and we were fortunate enough to have him only a short drive away. This felt like another practical reminder that God was taking care of us through these hard years.

Just after Logan turned three, he was healthy enough for his last kidney surgery, where they removed his non-functioning kidney and closed up the hole in his side. This procedure was the most painful and emotionally challenging of them all, but again, God reminded us He was with us through it.

Since then, by God's mercy, we have received mostly good news about Logan's health! He is seven now, and his remaining kidney is working so well that he doesn't need any medications, doesn't have any physical restrictions, and loves going to the beach! He enjoys playing baseball, basketball, and soccer, is getting taller by the day, excels at school, and doesn't seem any different from other kids his age. We still monitor certain things about his diet and activities, but most people don't even know he has any health issues at all.

None of Logan's journey has gone how I wish it would have, and unfortunately, it is not over. It is likely he will need a kidney transplant one day. Even still, I can never doubt God's faithfulness. He was there through the uncertainty of diagnosis and treatments; He was there in the tear-filled moments in hospital rooms, and He will be there for whatever is next. Even on the hardest days, we have confidence that no matter the outcomes, He was and is our hope in the midst of it, and we are never alone. The future is unknown. We don't know if or when Logan's condition will decline again, but we are certain that God will be with us every step of the way, no matter what happens.

Our family has been significantly changed by this journey, and we all carry scars that I wish were not there. When I look at Logan's physical scars on his body, I am reminded of the faithfulness of God, who was with us through the pain and who gave us hope in the darkness. I will never doubt the truth of Hebrews 10:23, which says, "Let us hold unswervingly to the hope we profess for he who promised is faithful."

In the years that followed, I realized just how thankful I was that I had this truth ingrained in me so deeply. I was grateful I could rest in His faithfulness when my second-born son was rushed to the hospital in an ambulance because of not being able to breathe. I was profoundly thankful for this hope when my husband was diagnosed with a rare and extremely aggressive form of cancer a couple of years later. Knowing that God is faithful was so comforting in those moments. My husband's cancer diagnosis felt like it knocked the wind out of us. It brought back all the fears from Logan's health challenges and forced us to wrestle with even harder questions. I had already come close to losing Logan as a baby; now I was faced with the possibility of losing my beloved husband. It was more than I could handle. His cancer journey pushed us all past our breaking points. It was the most intensely difficult time for our family, but what I can say confidently is that even on the hardest days, I was thankful I knew God would be faithfully with us, just like He had been before. We had hope in something so much greater than what was ahead, whatever the outcome.

My husband is thankfully cancer free now, and Logan's kidney is stable. We know this might not always be the case, but we celebrate the time we have together and regularly thank the Lord for the ways He has sustained us through the painful times. Their journeys are not over, and no matter what happens next or how their stories end, we know the One who gives us the greatest hope and who has promised to be with us always.

Glad I Didn't Know

I never imagined I would end up in so many intensely difficult situations that I would need constant reminders of God's nearness. He taught me about Himself when I was pushed to my limit and all I had was Him. I was in survival mode through Logan's early years, again through my husband's cancer battle, and through so many other things in between. It would have been too overwhelming to know what was in store for our family ahead of time, and I'm so glad God doesn't give us that information. I trusted God for one day at a time, and He was faithful to give me what I needed. While I am grateful to know these truths now, I would never repeat the journeys that brought me to this place if I had the choice. I am, however, grateful that God brings good out of hard things, just like He says he will do in James 1:2–5.

Lessons Learned

God is always faithful to keep His promises. I learned God doesn't promise an easy or comfortable life. He doesn't promise us good health. He doesn't promise us that we will get to enjoy many long years with our loved ones. The list of things I wish He promised but doesn't is long. But what God does promise is so much greater! He promises to be with us; we are never alone. Psalm 139:7–8 says, "Where shall I go from your Spirit? Or where shall I flee from your presence? If I ascend to heaven, you are there!" He promises hope when we face the scariest situations, as we see in Hebrews 6:18–19: "Therefore, we who have fled to him for refuge can have great confidence as we hold to the hope that lies before us. This hope is a strong and trustworthy anchor for our souls." I am thankful to know our God is a faithful God.[15]

---

15   Cari Arnold is a wife, a mom, and a professional in the insurance industry. Originally from Seattle, Washington, she attended Biola University, where she graduated with a BA in Psychology and now calls Southern California home. She and her husband, Jeff, met while doing ministry at their local church and remain actively involved today.

"Let us hold tightly without wavering to the hope we affirm,
for God can be trusted to keep his promises" (Hebrews 10:23).

Questions to Consider

- Thinking about hard seasons you have been through or are going through now, how can you see the Lord's nearness to comfort and sustain you through them? Consider asking Him for reminders and thank Him for them when He provides.

- What do you think would be too much to handle? The potential loss of a child, a spouse, a career, or a lifelong dream? Talk to the Lord about this.

- Is there something significant you have faced but know isn't completely resolved, and it still looms? How is the Lord using that to continue to show His faithfulness to you?

27

Me? International Board Member?

I received a call from a recruiter one day while serving as managing partner at the CPA firm. He wondered if I would be willing to consider a position on the board of World Vision. If you're not familiar with this organization, it is a global organization that works to help communities lift themselves out of poverty. It is one of the world's largest and most recognized nonprofits.

At the time of the call, our firm served over 1,000 nonprofit organizations. I have a heart for helping and only so many hours and so much funding, so I can't serve or give to everyone. It is important that someone is passionate about the organization if they are going to serve on the board. I was familiar with World Vision and their great work, but it hadn't been a passion of mine. I told the recruiter I would pray about it. I meant that. It wasn't just a stall tactic.

The recruiting process took about six months, and over that time, the Lord began to stir a passion inside me. I knew there was a board meeting in September, where they would vote on new board members. I was sitting at my desk one day and thought, *I really hope I'm able to join that board.* I realized then the Lord had provided the passion I needed to commit to service. The board chair called within a few days and welcomed me to the group. I was so excited!

I arrived at my first board meeting in January and seriously doubted my place. I looked around the table, and there was a former governor, a CFO of a major US corporation, leaders of national and international ministries, PhDs and MDs, and, and . . . you get the picture. In my mind, I reverted to being the kid who grew up outside of a town of 1,500 and who had only three in her graduating class. What was I doing here?

Each member of the board and the staff was so welcoming. They were genuinely glad to have me as part of the group. I was placed on the Finance Committee, which is a good place for a CPA. Over time, I realized the place I had and the value I could bring. Believe it or not, it isn't everyone's calling to serve in a finance role.

After serving there for a couple of years, I needed to step off because of a conflict of interest with the job I had taken. While I had prayed for passion before I joined the board, that same passion made it hard to leave. I was fully invested in the work being done and didn't want to leave the friends I had made and the ability to participate in meaningful discussions and decisions that impacted how work was done.

I was grateful when just one year later, my situation changed, and I was invited back to the board. This time, it was a more extensive role as it was not just to rejoin the US board but also become part of the international board. The same feelings started all over as I sat with people who spoke multiple languages, worked with individuals who overcame significant difficulties on a routine basis, and again who seemed so much more accomplished than me.

Having now served for a few years between World Vision US and World Vision International, I can see I do belong here. God prepared me for such a ministry just as He prepared the others in the room. I am incredibly humbled to be chosen to participate in this way and am privileged to serve with some incredibly godly leaders. I learn so much from them. Sometimes I am asked how I continue to develop professionally after twenty-five years in a profession, and I can assure you that these individuals contribute to that growth and development each time I have the pleasure of being with them.

Glad I Didn't Know

Wow! I am glad I didn't know I would serve in this capacity. First, it would have been too overwhelming. When you are called upon to do something, in the moment, you can step up. If you have years to think about it, you will find ways not to do it or worry yourself sick. Second, I probably would have messed up the entire thing. As you know by now, my planning can get in the way. I would have thought about the enormity of the role and then considered what education I needed to have, what professional experiences were necessary, and who I needed to network with along the way to be prepared for such an invitation. That's not what God had in mind.

Lessons Learned

I cling more and more to the saying, "God doesn't call the equipped. He equips the called." This chapter is a prime example of that. That phrase is exactly what I told the World Vision US Board when they elected me as board chair. I had become quite comfortable with my role on the board and the Audit and Finance Committee. The Lord loves to take me out of my comfort zone. I rely on Him more when I know I can't rely on myself.

> "Each of you should use whatever gift you have received to serve others, as faithful stewards of God's grace in its various forms" (1 Peter 4:10).

Questions to Consider

- Where are you called to serve now?

- Is there any place you are holding back because you don't believe you are _____ enough (good enough, smart enough, connected enough . . . you fill in the blank)?

- Have you ever looked back and been amazed at where you've ended up?

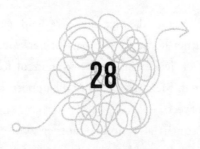

28

Caring for Family

Laura Whitley

I could not have known what lay ahead when I chose to leave an amazing thirty-four-year banking career to dedicate more time to family. At first, it was wonderful to finally have the time with my husband, John, to build the lake house of our dreams in which all our family and friends could gather, make memories, and celebrate milestones. Then my mother-in-law's physical and mental health began failing, and we spent much of our time taking her to doctors and hospitals and helping her to live as she wished—independently in the beautiful home John had built for her.

Ultimately, we had to make the difficult decision to move her to assisted living for the daily care she needed. Initially, she was angry and defiant, explaining she was ready to go home. We reminded her often that her home needed repairs before she could return and to enjoy this opportunity to make new friends.

After a few months, she realized what she lost in her home and her view of living alone she gained in new friendships and a simpler way of living, where all her needs were met. We held a multigenerational estate sale and sold her home to help pay for her care. Diagnosed with Alzheimer's, and then leukemia, we are so grateful for the loving care she is receiving now in Memory Care and the opportunity to visit her— although, it's bittersweet.

A couple of months after John's mother was settled, my father had another stroke, followed by a hip-breaking fall. Dad was eighty-seven years young, had recovered from two previous strokes, and his mind was still brilliant, so it was humbling for him to now need assistance in so many ways. It was difficult to see my strong Marine dad so vulnerable.

We were blessed to help care for him when he returned home from hip surgery for two weeks until he had a heart attack immediately followed by kidney failure. The ensuing four days in the hospital on hospice were as sacred as they were painful. When I asked him how he was feeling, he said, "Physically, I'm okay, but emotionally, it is difficult to say goodbye." Then he reminded us of the Marine motto: "The difficult we do immediately, the impossible takes a little longer." Saying goodbye proved to be impossible, so we let him know how much we loved him, that we would be with him again, and it was okay to go to heaven. He passed within days, surrounded by his loving family.

This season of sadness was followed by the next year starting joyfully as our oldest daughter got engaged to be married. Our family was healing and finally planning some fun celebrations! My mom came to visit to celebrate my brother's and sister-in-law's birthdays. The morning after the celebrations, Mom woke up nauseated and had difficulty breathing. She thought she'd eaten too much the night before. I sensed with great clarity that she was having a heart attack. Mom was eighty-three years young, incredibly healthy, throwing a fourteen-pound bowling ball several days a week in a league. So naturally, she fought as I insisted we go to the hospital. After immediate care, her heart attack was arrested. In the next few days, the underlying arrhythmia condition was diagnosed and a follow-up curing heart ablation surgery was scheduled. That surgery proved to be very successful. Hallelujah! The possibility of losing Mom so soon after Dad was absolutely overwhelming.

Meanwhile, one of the bright spots in our life, those wedding plans, continued until a month before the event when our daughter called off "the wedding of her dreams." She made a courageous and difficult decision to protect her health and serenity while her fiancé chose a different path. We surrounded her with love and support as she dealt with both the logistical and emotional upheaval that ensued. We frequently reminded her and ourselves that the details didn't matter. Making the right decision was important for now and for the future.

Glad I Didn't Know

During these beloved family heartaches and joys, I often felt like a child joyfully running across a pristine beach to dive into the ocean, only to discover I was swimming in a turbulent sea. One moment overcome by powerful crashing waves followed by brief reprieves as the tide receded. Waves still crash, wiping me out, but I have learned to pray, breathe, and function in between. I can't imagine surviving life's crashing waves without my Lord and Savior, Jesus Christ, continuous prayer, and the love and supportive prayers of so many dear Christ-followers.

I would like to protect myself and my family from the difficulties of life, but by not knowing what was ahead, I could face the current circumstances without becoming overwhelmed. I could take those breaths between waves and face the next one—sometimes even able to stop and enjoy the beauty of the beach and the ocean. Had I seen all that was ahead, it likely would have felt more like a tsunami, and I would have run for cover.

Lessons Learned

God has walked with me and carried me through it all. He has used me because I was available. That is my responsibility—to be available for what He has planned.

My prayers and those of so many faithful friends and family were repeatedly answered, although not always as we had expected or maybe wanted. This was another good reminder that just because a prayer wasn't answered according to my desire doesn't mean the Lord didn't listen or respond.

The last lesson is that God knows we sometimes need confirmation and validation that everything will be okay, and He is gracious to provide that. I'll return to my story briefly to further explain this lesson.

Shortly after my dad passed away, I woke at 3:00 in the morning and could clearly and loudly hear birds at the feeder outside. John keeps the bird feeder well stocked, but it was February and there shouldn't have been birds out . . . and it was the middle of the night, which is also not a time for birds. This realization all happened before I even opened my eyes. When I opened them, I was shocked by what I saw.

My dad was sitting on a park bench underneath a tree with birds all around him. He loved animals, so that was not surprising. "Dad, it's you," I said. He nodded. He looked to be in his thirties or forties. I said to him, "Your eyes are so blue, and you look so handsome."

Dad said three audible words, "Thank you, sweetheart," in his distinct voice. He had been injured during his military service and had shoulder problems. He couldn't wear a pullover shirt of any type, yet he had on a crewneck sweater.

I said, "I've never seen you in a pullover. You're not hurt anymore."

He smiled and nodded as if to say, "You're getting it."

That was where the vision ended. I immediately texted my brother so I wouldn't lose any of the details of the vision. I didn't want to wake my husband and run the risk of him thinking I had gone crazy. There was time to tell him later. To this day, though, I vividly remember the entire scene and appreciate how the Lord provided that as a means of comfort just when I needed it—both then and in the years to come.[16]

> "The Lord himself goes before you and will be with you; he will never leave you nor forsake you. Do not be afraid; do not be discouraged" (Deuteronomy 31:8).

Questions to Consider

- As an adult, what does "honor your parents" look like to you?

- Have you experienced a vision, or heard of others who have, which provided clarity or comfort about a situation?

- Are you part of the "sandwich generation" that is helping kids and parents navigate very different experiences? If so, what is the biggest challenge for you in doing so?

---

16   Laura Whitley is a transformational leader with expertise in building and managing global businesses. During her thirty-four-year career with Bank of America, she was president of Global Commercial Banking, Private Banking, and Consumer Banking Services, leading 30,000 teammates. She has been featured on CNBC and Bloomberg. Laura and her husband, John, reside in Dallas and are the proud parents of three wonderful young adults.

29

Transformation

I n 2022, I was headed to Guatemala to attend senior leadership team meetings for TEAM, the missions organization I was serving. I try to do as much as I can when I travel, and there is often overlap between multiple business connections or personal purposes, which allows me to utilize my time well. I reached out to a couple of leaders within World Vision International and asked if there was any way I could be an encouragement to the staff in Guatemala.

You should understand the culture within World Vision is one of the most engaging and gracious environments I have ever seen. Plans were quickly made for me to spend a day with them and included meeting with the Guatemalan board, meeting with local church leaders, taking part in a staff chapel, and being exposed to a variety of programs operating in the country.

I agreed to do what I thought was a simple devotion for their staff chapel time. I have done this in a number of other settings, and while it is somewhat out of my routine, I can prepare and feel adequately equipped to do this. However, the formal agenda arrived four days before my departure, and I suddenly felt *very* inadequate. It was scheduled to the minute and included an introduction, some music by a youth orchestra, and thirty-four minutes for a "Biblical Reflection," entitled "Transformational Development: Jesus at the Center" by Vonna Laue. That's me!!!

My immediate reaction was panic. Then I went into logistics mode. I emailed the board chair and asked if she had ever presented something like this before. The next day, she sent something, but I was only able to use a couple of paragraphs. Again, a sick and uneasy feeling swept over me. I realized I would be speaking English, and my words would be interpreted into Spanish. Great! That should mean I only needed seventeen minutes of content.

I finally got to where I should have started and prayed about it. The title itself was overwhelming. I'm a CPA, and this seemed like a dissertation for a doctoral study in Theology. As I calmed down and turned it over to the Lord, what I realized was that transformation in a community or in hundreds of communities around the world only happens when we are transformed by the life-giving power of Jesus. Not until we see personal transformation can we begin to see transformation around us or in the collective sense.

I went to work preparing. I referenced verses like Romans 12:1–2 and James 2:14–17. I spent some uninterrupted time and prepared what I thought was a pretty good reflection. I seldom rehearse any presentation I'm going to do but felt this was different and required a different type of preparation than I normally do. I rehearsed and timed the presentation. Ten minutes?! That was it! Back to the preparation. I expanded on additional ideas in James as the entire book discusses personal transformation. I completed my work on Sunday evening and revised it some on the plane on Monday.

I arrived at the first meeting early Tuesday morning with a sense of peace. The lady assigned as my interpreter was one of the first people I met. I told her how I had panicked about chapel but took comfort in knowing she would be interpreting, which would take time. She looked at me quizzically and said, "I interpret *while* you're talking." Everyone had a headset, and she would speak quietly into a microphone so they could hear her at the same time I was talking. There went my seventeen-minute idea! This time, I felt uneasy but quickly prayed and just turned it all back to the Lord again.

My time came to speak, and while I was nervous, I followed my prepared materials and finished thirty-three minutes later. I knew it was God's grace and God's message. As a few people thanked me for speaking about a topic that was extremely meaningful to them, I faithfully turned that praise and gratitude right back to the Lord and gave Him the credit. It had not been my intention, but it obviously had been His.

Glad I Didn't Know

If I had known in advance the length of time and the specific topic that would be assigned, I would not have agreed to present that day. I would have mentioned my lack of biblical training and my discomfort with something that I was not prepared or equipped to do. The Lord knew that and gave me no warning. The agenda was already prepared and disseminated to many people. I was committed without a graceful way to decline. That resulted in a "stretching exercise," which caused me to grow and trust Him in new ways.

Lessons Learned

What I found as I went through this process and in the several days that followed was that this idea of transformation kept coming up. It's like when you get a different car, the model and color of which you haven't seen before, but suddenly, you see it everywhere. As I studied and spoke about personal transformation, I started to see it everywhere. The Lord used the lesson I prepared to work in my heart; I learned my need for personal transformation paves the way for other kinds of transformation.

I thought, *Am I open to transformation, or do I panic when I see what is required?* I'm glad I got to sit in on my own "sermon."

> "Let the message of Christ dwell among you richly as you teach and admonish one another with all wisdom through psalms, hymns, and songs from the Spirit, singing to God with gratitude in your hearts" (Colossians 3:10).

Questions to Consider

- Were you ever scared to speak publicly and then it went well?

- If you had to give a devotion today, what would the topic be?

- How does transformation ring true in your life right now?

30

"I Cannot Walk"

Doug Batchelder

If we had planned our trip over the last fifteen months, we would have taken a detour. In retrospect, the journey "through the valley" was worth what we learned about God's gracious sufficiency.

On June 13, 2023, I answered the phone. Our thirty-four-year-old son was calling.

"Dad, I *cannot* walk . . ."

Those words began a journey into an unfamiliar valley we never anticipated.

Micah had what he thought was just a cold in May. After the symptoms subsided, he noticed his toes and fingers had begun to tingle. He mentioned it when he called Jane and me several times. The ER doctor (his regular doctor was unavailable) told him it was just a virus, and he would be better in a few days. However, he became dramatically worse.

The hand and foot tingling became numbness and increasing weakness. Micah went to the emergency room for a second time and was told again to go home—he would be better in a week or so. However, he worsened still. The weakness grew. Going up and down stairs at home where he and his wife, Souand, and their six-month-old baby, Eleanor, lived, became difficult. Walking became nearly impossible. Then one day, he fell, and it took Souand and a neighbor to pick him up.

That is when he called: "Dad, I *cannot* walk, but I don't want to go back to the ER. We waited five hours each time, and I can't do that again."

I told him, "Call 9-1-1 and go by ambulance. You will jump ahead of the curve without having to wait. This is no virus."

Micah entered Johns Hopkins Hospital, Howard County's campus that day. He would not leave the Johns Hopkins Hospital system for almost five months. The weakness spread upward from his feet and hands. Within days, he'd become a quadriplegic—unable to move his legs or arms. Prayer networks around the world began to pray for Micah around the clock. Churches, my colleagues at TEAM—a global ministry—family, friends, social media networks, and neighbors all prayed; it was a global concert of prayer.

The diagnosis: Guillain-Barré syndrome (GBS), a rare disease that causes numbness, weakness, and pain. GBS is precipitated by some unrelated infection, like a cold, to which your immune system overreacts, viewing your nerves as part of the infection and attacking them. Nerves, like wires, have insulation (myelin) around them, which functions to speed the electrical signals from the brain and spinal column to the rest of the body. GBS destroys the myelin, and in the most severe and rarest cases, GBS destroys the nerves themselves. That was Micah's situation.

Micah's feet and hands became completely numb. His skin elsewhere, when touched, felt like painful fire. His body lost temperature control. Paralysis spread up his limbs and torso, affecting his diaphragm, throat, larynx, tongue, facial muscles, and eyelids. His face looked like that of a stroke victim. He could not swallow without aspiration, and he developed pneumonia. A lobe in one lung collapsed. He needed oxygen, a feeding tube, and constant suctioning; he had IVs in both arms, and eventually, a central line to his heart, as he struggled to live and recover. He lost over fifty-five pounds, 25 percent of his body weight. Much of the loss was muscle tissue.

I drove to Maryland to stay at Micah's bedside to care for him. My wife, Jane, remained in New Jersey to assist with her ninety-six-year-old father's care, as he had experienced several severe falls requiring trips to the hospital. For weeks, Souand and I took turns sleeping in a recliner beside Micah, suctioning him every time he needed to swallow, day and night. Immunoglobulin therapy (IVIG) treatments began, giving him the antibodies of 100 healthy people, with the hope some of their antibodies would arrest the GBS. However, IVIG treatment ended with virtually no effect. His case was too severe.

The paralysis we observed on the outside was also happening on the inside, slowing digestion and, most seriously, affecting his diaphragm. Though he could inhale adequately, he could not exhale well enough to dispel the carbon dioxide (CO_2) properly. Though his oxygen levels remained satisfactory, his carbon dioxide levels continued to deteriorate to dangerous ranges. CO_2 levels are rated one to five, with five being the best. When Micah entered the hospital, his level had already declined to 2.7 and continued to drop. As Micah's condition weakened, I asked to speak to his neurologist alone.

"I can see Micah is growing worse and worse despite IVIG treatment. Doctor, I need to prepare my family for what lies ahead. So what can we expect?"

The doctor replied, "His CO_2 numbers are worsening. He is below two now. If it drops to one, it requires mandatory intubation. If the decline accelerates, intubation might not be enough. Below one, the patient falls asleep and never wakes up."

We were playing for keeps.

Because Micah's CO2 numbers continued to drop, he was transferred to the ICU at Bayview, the main campus of Johns Hopkins, in Baltimore. Each breath was an exhausting struggle. Coughing grew weaker and weaker. I called Jane and told her to come and to tell our five other children they needed to come to see Micah very, very soon. Micah's CO2 level had now fallen to 1.3. His condition was critical.

ICU is a lonely place, especially at night. Sitting in the dark beside my son, I kept a close eye on the monitors of his respiration, blood pressure, O2 levels, and heart rate. One night, he fell asleep and stopped breathing. I remembered the doctor's solemn words. I gently awakened Micah and told him, "Micah, you must breathe."

That night and the next, I thought we would lose him.

"I am so tired, Dad."

"I know. Just take the next breath."

"I want to see Mom and my brother and sisters," he barely whispered.

As I sat in the darkness, I thought of the many times as a pastor I had visited patients and families as a loved one lay near death in the hospital. As a pastor, you are needed to comfort those during their anguish. Now, there I was, in a strange city. No pastor nearby and my own pastor at home had recently resigned. It was a moment to be alone with God and tell myself all the things I had told others so many times before, throughout my thirty-five years of pastoral ministry: *God is sovereign. God is good.* The first truth without the second is terrifying, but welded together, those two truths provided me with a comfort that only comes from God's Spirit.

In the darkness of the ICU, I prayed, "Father in heaven, I love my son and don't want him to die. I would trade places with him, but I cannot. So I must trust him to both Your sovereignty and goodness. Please spare his life. Don't let him die, but if You choose not to save him, I will still trust that You are good, knowing Micah has trusted You as his Savior and he will be safe with You forever." Peace followed. Micah continued to breathe.

While most GBS patients respond well to immunoglobulin therapy (IVIG), Micah did not. IVIG probably kept his diaphragm from complete paralysis and saved his life. Otherwise, he did not improve. So the team of doctors recommended plasmapheresis—removing all antibodies and allowing his body to rebuild its immunology. After five treatments over ten days and, in answer to multitudes of prayers, Micah showed the first signs of improvement! GBS begins in the toes and fingers and works its way to the top of one's head. However, healing begins at the top of the head and slowly works its way to the fingers and toes as damaged nerves regrow one millimeter per day.

Inpatient physical and occupational therapy began, so Jane and I returned to New Jersey, and every Thursday evening, we drove the four hours back to see Micah and to relieve Souand. We continued this routine while he was in inpatient therapy. Jane, Micah, and I would pray before we left for New Jersey each week. One evening he prayed, "Dear Lord, I want to be well again so I can take care of my family." Tears streamed down his face and ours. His love for them motivated him.

Therapists helped Micah learn to walk and use his hands again. Then he contracted COVID-19 and was put in isolation for ten days. Most therapy stopped. We prayed he would not lose ground during isolation. Two of his therapists, Patty and Jessie, were so dedicated to his healing; they masked up and visited him in isolation to do some stop-gap therapy and teach him what he could do on his own. Ten days later, he was back in the therapy unit and received the best of care. From that point on, progress continued uninterruptedly, and he was discharged to home at the end of October. His mobility required a walker around the house and a wheelchair for longer distances. When not at the hospital, I worked at his home to make it as accessible as possible and to do the household chores he would normally do.

Micah continues to improve with therapy and will soon return to work, but he still needs to have feeling and strength restored to his feet. When the whole family gathered at Thanksgiving, he said, "I am a Thanksgiving miracle."

Micah's name means, "Who is like the Lord?" The answer is: *There is no one like Him. He is all we need.*

Glad I Didn't Know

Fifteen months ago, I did not know my ninety-one-year-old mom would have hip replacement surgery then fall and break her pelvis, that Jane's ninety-six-year-old father's health would decline precipitously, or that we would spend most of the summer and fall in Maryland, helping to care for Micah and his family—all while Jane and I were building a new home and moving! I'm glad I did not know how exhausting this extended year would be.

Lessons Learned

Knowing hundreds of people were praying for Micah, his family, and Jane and me is a powerful motivator to pray for others with boldness. Prayer works, and the prayers of God's people "accomplish much."

Answers to prayer motivate you to keep praying. Here are just a few answered prayers in Micah's story.

- God spared his life and is healing him.
- God gives strength for each day's challenges. His "manna" met our daily needs.
- Micah had a world-class team of physicians.
- Micah did not show discouragement or anger during the entire five months; instead, he expressed gratitude to each person who helped him, including those who cleaned his room.
- God provided skilled and encouraging therapists dedicated to his healing.
- God kept Souand safe while driving back and forth to the hospital and to work when she was completely exhausted. God kept

Jane and me safe in the thousands of miles we traveled between New Jersey and Maryland.
- Micah's, Souand's, and my employers were outstandingly kind while we were away from our jobs for weeks and weeks.
- Five months passed with him unable to move in bed, yet Micah never developed bed sores.
- The hospital provided a bed for Souand and baby Eleanor for the entire time, except when he was isolated, so they could encourage Micah by their presence.

When alone in a trial that tests your spiritual core, God and His truth are enough!

The comfort of others, while welcomed, is sometimes absent, but even though "we walk through the valley of the shadow of death, we can fear no evil," because He is Immanuel: "God with us."[17]

"Nothing in all creation is hidden from God's sight. Everything is uncovered and laid bare before the eyes of him to whom we must give account. Therefore, since we have a great high priest who has ascended into heaven, Jesus the Son of God, let us hold firmly to the faith we profess. For we do not have a high priest who is unable to empathize with our weaknesses, but we have one who has been tempted in every way, just as we are—yet He did not sin. Let us then approach God's throne of grace with confidence, so that we may receive mercy and find grace to help us in our time of need" (Hebrews 4:13–16).

17 Doug Batchelder has dedicated his life to public service. His career includes pastoring a church for thirty-five years, working in radio and television, a variety of leadership roles with the YMCA and in Christian education, public policy work, and global mission work. He has ministered on five continents and guest preaches often. Doug and his wife, Jane, raised six children and have four grandchildren. His passion is to be salt and light so others follow Jesus.

Questions to Consider

- How would your life change today if you were suddenly paralyzed? Be specific and think about all the implications.

- How would those changes be the same or different if it was your child, whether at home or grown?

- How have you seen the Lord answer specific prayers?

31

Run to Obey

Aaron Catlin

"What if I can sell it in a way that doesn't require us to pay a commission?" The question from my wife hung in the air for a moment; I was distracted by the NCAA basketball tournament game on the television that was being contested by my alma mater.

The distraction was real. After a couple of decades of easily forgotten seasons, my team had caught fire at the right time and was now threatening to make some serious noise during March Madness. Moving on to the Elite Eight? Big deal. Selling our new home in a somewhat down market without paying a sales commission in a pre-Zillow world? Unlikely. "Sure, that would be fine," I almost instinctively replied.

As I replay the events of that evening and the subsequent years in my mind, I'm both glad *for* and glad I didn't know what sort of wild chapter that seemingly innocuous exchange with my spouse would open up in our lives.

We were essentially living a version of the American Dream. We were involved with a great church that was growing rapidly, had two young daughters who were healthy and happy, enjoyed a job with seemingly endless opportunity, and had built a comfortable house on a wooded lot in the suburbs a couple of years earlier.

Much of our service in our local church revolved around cross-cultural ministry. We served on the missions committee and spent a significant portion of time meeting with college students who attended the medium-sized state university in the center of our city. Once a month, along with a few other families, we would prepare food, haul it to the international student center on campus, and host a meal for students to get to know them better and develop friendships that often led to invitations to our home and deeper conversations.

This sort of ministry involvement naturally led us toward the possibility of vocational cross-cultural work, but after several inquiries with various cross-cultural sending agencies and even an exploratory trip or two, we were convinced that our place was right there in the suburbs, packing up little kids and slow cookers full of halal foods, and traipsing across the city to serve dinner, attend basketball games, or lead Bible studies.

We often hosted international students in our home, which typically meant driving to both pick them up and drop them off, adding a good hour and a half of commuting time to our already full lives. We had occasionally discussed moving within walking distance of the campus to facilitate this ministry, but it wasn't a likely possibility, given the logistics of selling and my desire to only make profitable real estate decisions.

Flashing back to the basketball game: my wife listed our home on Craigslist, and a buyer almost immediately responded. The buyer had recently received an inheritance and was able to meet our asking price with cash and without negotiation. We had a contract within three days and closed in less than a month.

We purchased a beautiful century-old home half a block from campus, and students often popped in for meals, to shoot hoops, or to play ping-pong in the upper level of our two-story garage. While hosting an evening Bible study with a group of Asian and North American students, we became aware of the natural limitations of studying in a second language. Our young friends were eager to learn, but some concepts were hard to communicate or understand.

These were good years for our family. We knew our neighbors, developed deep relationships, and felt as though we were putting down the roots that would grow into a legacy of faith. Our small step of obedience to move had yielded fruit.

Now a family of five, I was driving two of my daughters to church one day while my wife remained home to care for an ill child. As I cruised over some rolling hills on the way to the service, I heard a message. I don't know that it was audible, but it was compelling and clear. I was convinced that God was prompting me to "learn Mandarin well enough to use it to make disciples." Yikes. I wanted to obey, but packing up a young family, leaving a fruitful life, and moving to the other side of the world is not a simple decision. I enrolled in an introductory language course at a local university and even enlisted a couple of my young Asian friends as language coaches and partners.

However, it soon became clear that full immersion in the language was the only viable way to learn it well enough to fulfill what I had been called to, as my classes and sessions with friends just didn't lead to proficiency. I worked with my firm to secure a position in Asia to use my business skills and experience to relocate internationally, but nothing seemed to be the right fit. Somewhat reluctantly, and then all at once, we took a leap. Within a year of that initial call to learn the language, our family had another baby, joined an international sending organization called TEAM, raised support while working full-time, sold all of our belongings, and sold our house at a significant loss.

Two weeks before departure, I took a final business trip to Chicago, handed off my remaining work responsibilities, and rode the subway to the consulate to pick up our passports with the visas for our new home securely glued inside. It was a lot to take in and process.

Glad I Didn't Know

I could write multiple chapters about all the things I was glad I didn't know at that time in my life. The next ten years unfolded in beautiful, complex, and sometimes difficult ways. I'm glad I didn't know just how challenging it would be to learn a difficult language, lose an identity as a competent and skilled communicator, live in one of the most densely populated districts of a densely populated country of the world, or that seemingly every aspect of everyday life would become a puzzle to solve.

Those difficulties changed us. There were some days, months, and even years that were brutal. Cross-cultural life and ministry often feel analogous to the curved lens of a magnifying glass. The lens works two ways, both magnifying and clarifying sin and insecurity while simultaneously concentrating heat and light and burning away competence. It leaves little of one's original identity.

Swimming in a sea of bygone competence and magnified frustration made me often question if I'd heard the Lord correctly or even if this supposed obedience was "worth it." Eventually, I saw the singeing caused by that cross-cultural magnifying lens as a kindness. He was using it to reveal and remove that which wasn't truly important. Measuring the worthiness or fruitfulness of an action or choice is a common, and very human, way to operate. However, I don't think it's very biblical or wise. It seems the Lord is much more interested in lead measures as opposed to my fascination with the lag side of the measuring stick.

Lessons Learned

I want to see the harvest; Jesus says to make sure the field is planted. I want to see the Kingdom come; Jesus says, "Take up your cross and follow me." I want my life to matter for something big and eternal; Jesus says the only way for that to happen is to lose this one.

Living in and for His Kingdom can feel upside down, backward, or both. However, if I believe He is Lord, then I have no other logical choice but to obey Him fully. Jesus is not the janitor of janitors, whistling and contentedly mopping up the results of my bad choices and messy decisions. Rather, He *is* the King of kings and the Lord of lords—with all power, honor, and glory owed to and belonging to Him. Kings give commands. Commands are not suggestions. They are meant to be obeyed.

Two things are clear: God has always been faithful. The Lord is never finished calling us to grow and stretch our faith in Him. In the past decade, we've moved to Asia, moved within Asia, started and grown a business, made disciples using that language we learned, moved back to the United States, and now find ourselves in an extraordinary but relatively unknown place in rural America, wondering, *What might be next?*

Know this: the Lord is sovereign, and the Lord is kind. He only calls us to do things that are for our ultimate and eternal well-being. Whatever that next step of obedience may be—for your good and His glory—run to obey![18]

> "Now an angel of the Lord said to Philip, 'Go south to the road—the desert road—that goes down from Jerusalem to Gaza.' So he started out, and on his way he met an Ethiopian eunuch, an important official in charge of all the treasury of the Kandake (which means "queen of the Ethiopians"). This man had gone to Jerusalem to worship, and on his way home was sitting in

---

18 Aaron Catlin served as a lobbyist, a communications specialist, and a consultant before his family moved and served overseas. Since returning to the US with his wife and four daughters, he continues to use his communications experience in a leadership role within TEAM, assisting the organization and other global workers in fulfilling the mission.

his chariot reading the Book of Isaiah the prophet. The Spirit told Philip, 'Go to that chariot and stay near it.'

"Then Philip *ran* up to the chariot and heard the man reading Isaiah the prophet. 'Do you understand what you are reading?' Philip asked.

"'How can I,' he said, 'unless someone explains it to me?' So he invited Philip to come up and sit with him" (Acts 8:26–31).

Questions to Consider

- Have you ever had a prompting from the Lord that just didn't seem like it made sense to obey?

- In instances where you've obeyed quickly, what was the result?

- Will you take five minutes right now to sit quietly and ask the Lord to remind or tell you how you can obey?

Seasons of Life

Sometimes things are sunny; spring is in the air, and there is great hope about what lies ahead. Summer finds us enjoying life in its fullest, soaking up the long days of sunshine. That's good because those times turn to fall, where it may not be difficult, but we know the colors are changing, the days are getting shorter, and there may be difficult times ahead. Growing up in South Dakota, I can relate to the harshness of winter, when some days you just have to struggle through the cold and isolation. The light is short. The dark is long. You yearn to see the return of spring and signs of life again.

I have found life to be that way. There are seasons. Sometimes life is going along well. Our relationships are blossoming, and there is a freshness to everything we experience. Sometimes it is dark and isolated, and we are not sure when we will see hope and joy again.

As I considered this one time in preparation for a devotion I was giving at work, I looked at the book of Psalms. We often go there for both comfort and encouragement. I examined each chapter, and here is what I found: Psalms 1 and 2 were encouraging. Psalms 3–7 were filled with angst. Psalms 8 and 9 were encouraging. Psalms 10–17 were filled with angst. Psalms 18–21 were encouraging. Psalm 22 was filled with angst. On and on this goes, back and forth through the entire book. Overall, there are eighty-five encouraging Psalms and sixty-five related to the trials of life and battling a downtrodden spirit.

There is one span of ten Psalms of rejoicing and one span of twelve Psalms of mourning. Otherwise, they stretch shorter amounts, but each emotion is always followed by the other. It creates this rhythm, which we experience in life too. This should keep us grounded and realistic when times are great.

Maybe you just got engaged or have a new job. The world seems as if it couldn't be better. That's fantastic! Enjoy this season and rejoice in the blessings you are currently experiencing, but also be aware that it won't last forever. Keep grounded in the Word and continue to develop your relationship with Christ because there will be a winter season coming.

Maybe you just received a cancer diagnosis. While that is traumatic by itself, you and your spouse may have recently encountered a corporate downsizing, and your income is less than half of what it was previously. The days are dark and isolation is setting in if you don't guard your heart. Allow others into your life and continue to seek the Lord even when He seems distant and seems as if you're talking in an echo chamber. You can't see it, but spring will come. Daylight hours will increase, and gray skies will give way to sunshine. Keep going!

I'm a sports fan, and I often think it would be helpful if we could see life from the upper deck like at a football game. When you are on the field and carrying the ball, all you see are the great big defensive players headed your way. What you don't see are your teammates, ready to block each one of those big scary guys, or maybe the other teammate who is following you, ready to pick up the ball if you happen to drop it. There is a greater plan. You are one of twenty-two people on the field and you have to do your job even when you can't see the big picture, but rest assured, there is someone who sees the whole field and knows the end result.

Glad I Didn't Know

I'm glad I don't know exactly when the seasons will change. If I knew when that would happen, I would undoubtedly try to manage it. My life would be filled with more anxiety because I would try to control those things that are outside my control.

Lessons Learned

Anticipate better days and soak them up when they come. Allow God to be God and rest in His omniscience.

> "Therefore do not worry about tomorrow, for tomorrow will worry about itself. Each day has enough trouble of its own" (Matthew 6:34).

Questions to Consider

- What season of life are you currently experiencing?

- Should you prepare for the next season or focus on gaining all you can from this one?

- Is there someone who needs you to be a good teammate in their life right now and block for them or pick up a dropped ball?

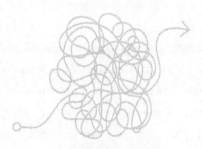

Conclusion

As you have walked the journey of many stories that show why people are glad they didn't know, you've been asked to consider your life in numerous ways. What are you glad you didn't know? Can you see those circumstances in both challenges and unexpected blessings?

It's interesting how most people I meet will say they learned the most or grew the most spiritually during difficult times. I've never had someone say something that fell into their lap or came easily to them taught them much.

Why do we seek to avoid the difficulties? We don't like pain, but we like the results. I think the Christian life is similar to going to the gym. It's not easy. Many days you wake up and think, *Not today*, but when you push through day after day, you see the results.

As I encouraged you in the introduction, I will remind you in the conclusion: please consider making your own **Glad I Didn't Know** list that highlights those difficult challenges and unexpected blessings you are glad you didn't know. Think about the lessons learned and what you might have missed out on if you had known them in advance.

There are certain things I have encountered later in life that I realized I can face only because I know the Lord has been faithful before and I can count on Him today. May that be more true to you now than ever before.

I'll end with this simple, yet difficult, admonition from Scripture: "Rejoice always, pray continually, give thanks in all circumstances; for this is God's will for you in Christ Jesus" (1 Thessalonians 5:16–18).

I would love to hear your **Glad I Didn't Know** story. If you would like to share it, please feel free to send it to gladididntknow@gmail.com.

Acknowledgments

To the professionals at Morgan James Publishing: I'm thankful you saw value in this project and were willing to bring it to life. I'm especially grateful for Terry Whalin and his encouragement and support from the beginning and for responding so promptly and thoroughly no matter what questions I had.

To my editor, Cortney: You didn't just edit, you polished. Thank you for keeping my voice and making it better. I was scared to open your first edits but shouldn't have been because you were gracious and every suggestion was valuable.

To the incredible group of people who contributed stories: You are noted throughout the book where your story was included. Thank you for making this possible. Without you, it is just one person's perspective that can easily be disregarded by the reader. Your stories show a pattern of the Lord's faithfulness that is indisputable. We all have challenges and unexpected blessings. Thank you for your vulnerability and willingness for the Lord to use what you've learned to bless others.

To my friends and colleagues at World Vision and TEAM: I pray this book will be a blessing to your incredibly valuable ministries. I'm blessed to spend my time supporting organizations like yours that invest themselves in providing life in all its fullness to children and sending disciples who make disciples. Thank you for what each of you do daily and for letting me be a part of it.

To Leith, Rich, Tami, and Justin: Thank you for being willing to put your name on this project with your endorsement. When we talk about unexpected blessings, I consider your involvement in my life exactly that.

To my family: Bryan, I'm sure you wonder when I take on yet another project like this one, but you are the reason I can do what I love and live the crazy life I live. You give me the encouragement and support to make it all possible. Bethany and Kimberly, you have both overcome significant adversity in life, but through all of it, you have shown hearts for others that challenges me to love better. I'm so proud of the godly young women you have become. Your contributions to this book and your encouragement were instrumental in *Glad I Didn't Know* becoming a reality. I told you as you were growing up that I was your mom and not your friend. As you have transitioned into adulthood, I love being both now! Andrés, you show genuine interest in whatever others are doing and make them feel valued because of it. David, you make Nonna smile, no matter what might be happening or however busy I am.

About the Author

Vonna Laue was raised in South Dakota and never imagined the opportunities that lay ahead. She received her Bachelor's Degree in Accounting from Black Hills State University and an MBA from the University of Colorado at Colorado Springs.

Vonna writes for various publications, speaks at regional and national conferences, and has assisted in developing various training programs. She loves serving churches and ministry organizations in operational areas and does so through consulting and board roles. She has been in all fifty states, twenty-plus countries, and 111 airports and counting.

She has an amazing husband, two fabulous daughters, a fantastic son-in-law, and an adorable grandson. She loves the beach, watching sports, and traveling with her husband in this season of life, which they describe as #thriving.

Our vision for every child, life in all its fullness.
Our prayer for every heart, the will to make it so.

World Vision®

WHO WE ARE AND HOW WE SERVE

World Vision is a Christian humanitarian organization dedicated to working with children, families, and their communities worldwide to reach their full potential by tackling the causes of poverty and injustice. Motivated by our faith in Jesus Christ, we serve alongside the poor and oppressed as a demonstration of God's unconditional love for all people. We provide hope and assistance to communities through our presence in nearly 100 countries, serving everyone in need regardless of religion, race, ethnicity, or gender.

WAYS TO GET INVOLVED

Invest in a child.

Child sponsorship is a personal way to show God's love to a child in need. Your monthly gift is combined with those of other sponsors to support community-wide projects that empower your child, their family and community, and other vulnerable kids to rise above poverty for good. Because of our community-focused solutions, for every child you help, four more children benefit, too. Sponsor today at worldvision.org.

Equip families and communities to thrive.

Your gift to the World Vision Fund will help meet critical needs both today and tomorrow, helping people in some of the world's toughest places to rebuild in the wake of disasters and empowering entire communities to lift themselves out of poverty. You'll help kids and families tackle the big issues that keep them in poverty, equipping them to thrive with reliable access to basics like clean water, nutrition, healthcare, education, and more. Give today at worldvision.org/donate.

team

The year is 1890. A British missionary named Hudson Taylor, who had risen to some measure of notoriety in the world, calls upon the Church to send 1,000 missionaries to China. The call went out, and many heard it. A few answered, dedicating their lives from that point forward to planting the seeds of the gospel in a land far from their own. Another man committed to mobilizing and sending 100 of the called-for number.

That commitment to partnership and obedience birthed an organization called TEAM. Origin stories are important and helpful because they ground, inspire, and remind us of truth north in purpose. For more than 130 years, God has allowed TEAM to continuously minister around the world to *partner with the global church in sending disciples who make disciples and establish missional churches to the glory of God.*

More than thirteen decades later, TEAM continues on this path of obedience. While the crux of the mission remains the same, much has changed. The global Church is no longer primarily composed of disciples from Europe or North America; in fact, 80 percent of the Church now resides outside the traditional West.

Each of us has a duty and delight to participate in the call to make disciples of all nations. Learn more about what your part might be at www.team.org.

A free ebook edition is available with the purchase of this book.

To claim your free ebook edition:

1. Visit MorganJamesBOGO.com
2. Sign your name CLEARLY in the space
3. Complete the form and submit a photo of the entire copyright page
4. You or your friend can download the ebook to your preferred device

Morgan James BOGO™

A **FREE** ebook edition is available for you or a friend with the purchase of this print book.

CLEARLY SIGN YOUR NAME ABOVE

Instructions to claim your free ebook edition:
1. Visit MorganJamesBOGO.com
2. Sign your name CLEARLY in the space above
3. Complete the form and submit a photo of this entire page
4. You or your friend can download the ebook to your preferred device

Print & Digital Together Forever.

Snap a photo

Free ebook

Read anywhere

Printed in the USA
CPSIA information can be obtained
at www.ICGtesting.com
JSHW080024071124
73101JS00010B/282